Flexible Integration:
Towards a More Effective and
Democratic Europe

Monitoring European Integration 6

Centre for Economic Policy Research

The Centre for Economic Policy Research is a network of over 300 Research Fellows, based primarily in European universities. The Centre coordinates its Fellows' research activities and communicates their results to the public and private sectors. CEPR is an entrepreneur, developing research initiatives with the producers, consumers and sponsors of research. Established in 1983, CEPR is a European economics research organization with uniquely wide-ranging scope and activities.

CEPR is a registered educational charity. Institutional (core) finance for the Centre is provided by major grants from the Economic and Social Research Council, under which an ESRC Resource Centre operates within CEPR; the Esmée Fairbairn Charitable Trust; the Bank of England; 17 other central banks and 40 companies. None of these organizations gives prior review to the Centre's publications, nor do they necessarily endorse the views expressed therein.

The Centre is pluralist and non-partisan, bringing economic research to bear on the analysis of medium- and long-run policy questions. CEPR research may include views on policy, but the Executive Committee of the Centre does not give prior review to its publications, and the Centre takes no institutional policy positions. The opinions expressed in this report are those of the authors and not those of the Centre for Economic Policy Research.

Published by CEPR, 25–28 Old Burlington Street, London W1X 1LB
© Centre for Economic Policy Research
British Library Cataloguing in Publication Data
A Catalogue record for this book is available from the British Library

ISBN: 1 898128 22 7

Contributors

Mathias Dewatripont
ECARE, Université Libre de Bruxelles, and CEPR

Francesco Giavazzi
IGIER, Università Bocconi, and CEPR

Jürgen von Hagen
Universität Mannheim, Indiana University, and CEPR

Ian Harden
University of Sheffield

Torsten Persson
Institute for International Economic Studies, Stockholm University, and CEPR

Gérard Roland
ECARE, Université Libre de Bruxelles, and CEPR

Howard Rosenthal
Princeton University

André Sapir
ECARE, Université Libre de Bruxelles, and CEPR

Guido Tabellini
IGIER, Università Bocconi, and CEPR

Contents

List of tables

List of figures

Foreword

This report was prepared in anticipation of the 1996 Intergovernmental Conference. Its goal is to explore the advantages and limits of flexible integration, a consistent framework enabling the European Union to meet the challenges of the next steps of European integration effectively and successfully. By emphasizing analysis rather than specific proposals, our hope is to stimulate discussion and provide a basis for political debate that avoids deadlock at the Intergovernmental Conference.

Members of our group have different views about the future of Europe. Some conceive flexible integration as a method to overcome medium-term obstacles to building a European Union based on long-term goals common to all members. André Sapir, who tends to favour multispeed over flexible integration, is particularly concerned that the latter would be too flexible and end up being a glorified form of 'Europe *à la carte*' unless a supranational body (like the European Commission) played a more central role. Others see flexible integration as an open-ended arrangement accommodating diversity within the European Union. We all see flexible integration as a way to achieve a more effective and democratic European Union.

In writing this report we have benefited from helpful discussions with numerous individuals. Among them, we wish to thank particularly Alan Dashwood and the participants in a seminar held in June 1995. We thank Paul De Grauwe, Carl Hamilton, Alexis Jacquemin, Assar Lindbeck, Frank Vibert and Richard Portes for valuable comments on an earlier draft. Giovanni Guazzarotti provided able research assistance; Nancy De Munck, Romy Genin and Roxy Glaze deserve our thanks for excellent secretarial assistance. The responsibility for the views presented in this report remains, of course, ours alone.

Preface

Informed discussion of European integration should be based on economic analysis which is rigorous, yet presented in a manner accessible to public- and private-sector policy-makers, their advisers and the wider economic policy community. These are the objectives and the intended readership of CEPR Reports.

Monitoring European Integration assesses the progress of and obstacles encountered by economic integration in Europe. A rotating panel of CEPR Research Fellows meets periodically to select key issues, analyse them in detail, and highlight the policy implications of the analysis. The output of the panel's work is a short annual Report, for which they take joint responsibility. This is the sixth in the series.

CEPR is a network of over 300 economists based in over 100 different institutions, primarily in Europe. Much of the research in the Centre's various programmes relates to short- and long-run issues of economic policy in Europe. CEPR puts extremely high priority on effective dissemination of both policy research and the fundamental research underlying it. This series of annual Reports has become an important component of this effort.

The topic for this Report is the set of choices that will dominate both political and economic debate in Europe over the next year and more: what does the construction of Europe require from the European construction? In other words, what is the best way to (re)organize and structure the Union's institutions to achieve its political and economic objectives? Our authors approach this immense challenge with a fresh view from *political economy*: their analysis focuses on the requirements of economic integration and their political expression; and they use the tools of modern political economy as well as political science and law. The prescience, analytical clarity and relevance of previous Reports in this series promise a fresh, illuminating approach, and I believe readers will find these expectations justified.

The 1990 Report examined the impact of developments in Eastern Europe on the economies of Western Europe and on the process of economic integration among them. Some of its key insights went against conventional (and even new) wisdom, yet have proved correct and prophetic – for example, the conclusion that German unification would entail a real appreciation of the DM in the short run.

The 1991 Report dealt with Economic and Monetary Union in the European Community, in particular the macroeconomic and microeconomic issues arising from the process leading to a single currency and a European Central Bank. The Report has served as a guide to evaluating the Maastricht Treaty and as a text for interpreting developments in the EMS since August 1992. Again, the analysis in that Report has proved far-sighted and robust, in particular its concerns with the problems of transition to monetary union.

The 1992 Report analysed the political economy of enlargement of what is now the European Union. The Report argued that the issues raised by the EFTA countries' wish to move immediately from the European Economic Area to full EU membership were primarily political; whereas for the existing EU members, the motivation was reversed – the EEA had been mainly a political gesture, but there were significant economic incentives for bringing the EFTAns into the Union. The weakness of the economic motivation for the EFTAns may help to explain the difficulty of gaining popular support for accession in these countries. The picture for the Central and East European Countries (CEECs) was and remains quite different: on economic grounds, EU membership is not realistic for some time to come; but radically improved access to EU markets (including agriculture) is essential for the economic progress necessary to make membership feasible.

The fourth MEI Report, on subsidiarity, will serve for a long while as the fundamental study of this complex problem of political economy. It examines the application of the principle of subsidiarity to both the macroeconomic and the microeconomic policies of the Union. It shows where central intervention may be justified on economic grounds and where there is no such justification, although political and bureaucratic motivations may nevertheless result in intervention.

MEI 5 offers a new approach to the challenge of high unemployment in Europe. The Report argues that the repeated calls for deregulation as the solution to European unemployment are oversimplified and naive: the costs of regulation are not as high as they appear, nor are European labour markets as sclerotic as is commonly argued, nor are the differences with the United States as clear as conventional wisdom maintains. This naivety extends to the politics of high unemployment: European societies simply do not appear ready, according to the Report, to sacrifice the advantages of high wages, benefits and job protection in order to fight high unemployment. The authors analyse this resistance to solutions and what *can* be done with incremental change.

The German Marshall Fund of the United States has again provided generous financial assistance essential to the completion of the Report. We are also grateful to the UK Department of Trade and Industry; to the Foreign and Commonwealth Office; to the Commission of the European Communities, whose Human Capital and Mobility programmes financed the Centre's research network on 'Macroeconomics, Politics and Growth in Europe'; and to the Ford Foundation, which has supported much of the Centre's research on economic integration. This Report includes new research, but since it is written and published quickly so as to be relevant to ongoing policy processes, it must rest on a solid base of past fundamental and policy-oriented research. The authors and CEPR express their continuing thanks for the support of such research which has come from these bodies and all others that contribute to the Centre's funding.

The authors and CEPR are also grateful to officials in several countries and in the European Commission who were generous with their time and cooperation in discussing the issues treated here. For the production of the Report they thank Julie Deppé and James MacGregor, as well as other staff at CEPR whose patience and professionalism have been most helpful.

None of these institutions or individuals is in any way associated with the content of the Report. The opinions expressed are those of the authors alone, and not of the institutions to which they are affiliated nor of CEPR, which takes no institutional policy positions. The Centre is extremely pleased, however, to offer to an outstanding group of European economists this forum for economic policy analysis.

Richard Portes
20 September 1995

1   Europe at a crossroads

The early 1990s was a unique period of hope and expectations for Europe. The Single Market was about to be completed. The Maastricht Treaty was in preparation and the European Monetary System (EMS) seemed likely to evolve naturally into a single European currency. Enlargement of the European Union was imminent, with several countries knocking at the door, eager to become members. The collapse of the iron curtain added new and previously unimaginable dimensions to the vision of an integrated Europe, to be built on the cornerstones of democracy, peace and market economy. Europe seemed to be heading for a transformation of historic significance.

Then came the cold showers. The Maastricht Treaty was poorly received by public opinion. The EMS nearly collapsed under pressures from financial markets in 1992 and 1993. Economic recession further increased an already high unemployment rate, reminding policy-makers of their failure to solve Europe's most pressing social problem. War in the former Yugoslavia and political instability in the former Soviet Union drew attention both to the fragility of the new international political order and to Europe's inability to formulate a coherent foreign policy. All of this has changed the political climate in the European Union dramatically. The Union itself no longer seems such a successful model and, to many, its institutions appear flawed.

Europe is now at a crossroads. Opportunities for further integration and enlargement are still there, but it is widely agreed that the present European institutions are inadequate to meet the challenges that these opportunities present. Four pressing challenges concern the size, the scope, the depth and the legitimacy of European integration. The natural forum to tackle these challenges is the intergovernmental conference that is scheduled to begin in 1996.

1.1 The challenges ahead

1.1.1 Enlarging the Union

The first challenge is posed by the increasing size of the Union. The existing European institutions are, by and large, those designed for the original Community of six states. That Community was relatively homogeneous, economically as well as politically. Today the Union has 15 member states, with significantly different economies and political systems. Many nations at the Union's eastern rim, and some at its southern rim, expect to become members in the years to come. If they do, the Union will have 10–15 additional member states, giving it even greater economic and political diversity. The Union cannot seriously envisage such a further increase in its size without major institutional reform. Enlargement to, say, 25 countries under the current rules would make the Commission, the Council and the Parliament dysfunctional, and severely impair their decision-making capacity.

Prospects of enlargement also put a question mark over two activities that together account for 80% of the EU budget: the Common Agricultural Policy (CAP), and the Structural Funds that subsidize infrastructure and capital investment in Europe's poorer regions. Applying the CAP and Structural Fund rules mechanically to the prospective members of Central and Eastern Europe would require doubling the EU budget. Political difficulties provoked by previous attempts to increase the budget suggest that scaling up the programmes in this way would meet strong opposition. But scaling them down would also trigger strong opposition from their current beneficiaries. Enlargement, therefore, has to involve fundamental renegotiation of the *status quo*.

Enlargement may be problematic, but postponing it is risky. The transition of former Soviet-style societies to free market economies is not yet successful and the transition to political democracies not yet irreversible. Excluded from the prosperity and freedom of Western Europe for decades, the citizens of these countries are now eager to stabilize their young democracies by joining the European Union. It is in the interests of all current EU members to secure peace and stability at the Union's borders. Postponing enlargement would just create greater uncertainty for all European countries in the era that has succeeded the cold war.

1.1.2   Widening the scope of integration

A second challenge is the scope of the Union. At present, all member states share a unique body of legislation and commitments, the so-called *acquis communautaire*. The *acquis* embodies a delicate balance of gains and sacrifices for each state and is, in effect, a contract between the members of the Union. Any widening of the scope of integration adds to the *acquis* and so alters the existing balance of gains and losses for all the parties to the contract. This makes agreement on widening difficult to achieve.

Some member states now want to extend the scope of common policy-making to new areas, such as foreign and security policies. Other states are unwilling to accept these proposals. Future enlargement of the Union can only exacerbate such tensions, as member states will be even more diverse economically and politically and differ even more in their objectives.

Disagreement over the scope of integration also results in confusion about the division of responsibility between the Union and the states. An example is the attitude of citizens towards the unemployment problem. The prominence of EU institutions in some economic fields perhaps makes it natural for citizens to blame Brussels for European unemployment, even though labour market policy is almost exclusively within the competence of member states. Seeing the blame fall on Brussels may be convenient for national governments, but evading responsibility for problems that have predominantly domestic origins cannot be a viable or desirable long-run option for national governments in this or any other policy area.

1.1.3   Deepening existing integration

The third major challenge concerns the depth of integration. In the areas of Union competence, there has been only a limited transfer of national sovereignty to the EU. This leads to problems with enforcement and efficacy. First, the Union itself has only limited sanctions available and cannot rely on the ultimate threat of force. It must, therefore, rely mainly on member states to put EU law and policy into effect. Implementing the Single Market, in particular, depends on action by national administrations. Unsurprisingly, many Union directives get incorporated into national legislation only very slowly, or not at all. Even when they have been incorporated, national enforcement of the directives is often lax and uneven. Lax enforcement undermines the working of the Single Market. Failure to realize the vision of a European-wide market may ultimately put the whole credibility of the EU institutions at stake. Being serious about enforcement is therefore vital. Serious enforcement is very difficult, however, because measures must then be directed against national governments, which are themselves key actors and decision-makers in the Union.

Second, the intergovernmental mode of integration can cause problems with efficacy of decision-making in the Council, where many decisions still require unanimous agreement. Under the unanimity rule, states can threaten to veto agreements in one area of European cooperation in order to obtain concessions in other, perhaps unrelated, areas. Efficient decisions cannot be taken, or they may require decision packages, where unanimity is bought by inefficient 'side payments'; these can be policy concessions that produce discontent among citizens in other countries, or transfer programmes that cause economic inefficiencies. Further enlargement will make this kind of 'hostage taking' an even more serious problem.

The curious legal framework of the EU aggravates the efficacy problem. Unlike nation states, the Union does not have a normal constitutional hierarchy of law, with constitutional safeguards and rules about rule-making at the top, ordinary laws further down and administrative regulations at the bottom. Although Union institutions have powers to make rules and decisions of various kinds, the Treaties themselves also contain detailed provisions that really belong to the categories of ordinary law or administrative regulation, rather than constitutional law. This tends to stigmatize change and produce unnecessary gridlock when circumstances call for specific rules to be altered. The lack of a legal hierarchy, combined with the need for national enforcement, leads to the practice of writing EU rules in great detail. Detailed EU regulations tend to become the object of public ridicule: witness the publicized regulation of the proper shape of bananas and the colour of fire extinguishers.

The enforcement and efficacy problems have led some states to push for deeper European integration. Proposals to use majority rule for a larger set of Union decisions are perhaps the clearest expression of this impetus. Other states oppose deepening, fearing that it would seriously threaten national sovereignty. Enlargement of the EU and a wider scope of integration would add to their fears of being overruled by majority views in more and more areas of economic and political life.

1.1.4   Closing the democratic deficit

Last but not least, a burning issue is the legitimacy of the EU institutions. So far these institutions have worked remarkably well, but the complaints about a democratic deficit reflect growing public discontent with the Union. The democratic deficit relates mainly to the two most important Union institutions: the Commission and the Council.

The Commission largely controls what is discussed and decided in the Union. Even though many policy initiatives originate in the Council, it is the Commission's exclusive right to initiate proposals for Union legislation. This right allows the Commission to set a key part of the Council's agenda and gives it a powerful influence on the amendments that the European Parliament can make to Council proposals. The Commission is also the body that is supposed to enforce most of the Union's common policies. Relative to these extensive powers, the Commission's accountability to the public is very limited.

Although it is the main decision-making body in the EU, the Council is only indirectly accountable to citizens. A change of majority in a national parliament that causes a change of government automatically leads to a change of national ministers in the Council. However, national elections span too wide a range of issues to work well as an accountability mechanism for Council decisions. The secrecy surrounding the Council's deliberations and decisions also makes it hard to exercise accountability. The European Parliament is the only directly elected European institution (since 1979), but its general powers are slim compared with those of the Council and the Commission. Its control of the Commission does not extend beyond approval and censure of the body as a whole. In sum, the Council's predominance and the Parliament's circumscribed powers make the democratic accountability of the Commission very limited.

No less important for the democratic deficit is the mode of decision-making in the Council. A continued trend away from unanimity towards majority voting in the Council seems inevitable, since there is no other way to avoid a paralysis of decision-making which would itself discredit the EU institutions. This trend will weaken the indirect democratic control that national parliaments may exercise over Council decisions by controlling their national representative in the Council. As a result, the Council will have progressively less legitimacy than if it were chosen by direct democratic procedures.

Another important aspect of the democratic deficit is that existing EU institutions are biased towards coalition formation between countries and do not invite enough coalition formation across – rather than along – national borders. Indeed, decision-making in the Council only allows for coalitions between countries and excludes border-cutting coalitions on issues where interests naturally aggregate across national borders. An example is industrial policies, where European consumers form a natural, but unrepresented, coalition against the interests of national industries. It is true that the Commission operates like an 'advocate' for Europe, as Commissioners are supposed to defend the general European interest through the initiatives of the Commission. But the Commission's lack of legitimacy weakens its power as an advocate for pan-European interests. Since each country has at least one post, Commissioners implicitly become advocates of national interests in the eyes of the national governments which nominate the candidates.

The lack of a hierarchy of law also contributes to the democratic deficit. The legal framework of the Union has become unintelligible to most people, with the result that the European public has no clear understanding of the basic values and principles enshrined in the Treaties. It is likely that this confusion contributes to the unrealistic public view that the Union should solve economic problems even in fields where either it lacks the legal right to act, or it possesses no effective policy instruments. The confusion may also fuel the common caricature in the European press of a Commission full of power-hungry bureaucrats engaged in excessive regulation.

1.2 The agenda for the future of Europe

The objectives of the EU are political as well as economic. Article A of the Treaty on European Union (the Maastricht Treaty) states: 'the determination of the member states to continue the process of creating an ever closer union among the peoples of Europe'. Article B defines the five specific objectives of the Union, which are both economic and political: 'to promote economic and social progress ... through the creation of an area without internal frontiers, through ... economic and social cohesion and through ... economic and monetary union ...; to assert its identity on the international scene ... through ... a common foreign and security policy ...; to strengthen the protection of the rights and interests of the nationals of its Member States through ... citizenship of the Union; to develop close cooperation on justice and home affairs; to maintain in full the *acquis communautaire* and build on it...'.

In conformity with the Maastricht Treaty a conference with government representatives will convene in 1996 to examine those provisions of the Treaty for which revision is provided, in accordance with the objectives set out in Articles A and B. There is a proposed agenda for the 1996 intergovernmental conference (IGC). It is still too early to predict the actual agenda, let alone the outcome, of the IGC, but different scenarios can be envisaged.

Current tensions and problems inside the EU may make the IGC's deliberations go on for a long time, perhaps years, only to produce minor results that will seem insignificant to EU citizens. Such a scenario would entail enormous risks for the viability of the Union. Protracted negotiations, leading to cosmetic changes that do not address the real challenges facing Europe, would further discredit the Union in the eyes of the public. Enlargement to include Central and Eastern Europe would be postponed. This delay would bring additional uncertainties, with no compensating reduction in the risks attached to the eventual accession of new members. When enlargement finally takes place, careful compromises built over decades among fewer and more homogeneous states might unravel, jeopardizing the gains achieved in European integration and bringing an end to decades of prosperity and stability.

Another possible scenario is for a less protracted IGC, producing minor Treaty changes aimed mainly at the completion of the final stage of Economic and Monetary Union (EMU). This would mean adding sufficient new supranational elements to the constitutional structure of the Union to satisfy Germany – in return for abandoning the Deutschmark – but retaining a sufficient degree of intergovernmentalism to satisfy France, the country that seems to care most about EMU. The changes could also partly tackle the accountability problem, by giving greater power to the European Parliament or to the European Court of Justice. Such changes, however, would not be sufficient to deal with the challenges that Europe now faces. Conflicts between proponents and opponents of widening and deepening would remain. These tensions would become more pressing as candidates for membership knock more loudly on the door. Another IGC would have to be called within a few years.

There is also a third possibility – the one we want to advocate – of a far more radical scenario that attempts to meet the challenges faced by the EU head on. To handle these challenges the IGC would attempt to introduce more flexibility and more opportunities for choice, compared with the existing approach to integration built on multispeed adoption of a fixed *acquis communautaire*. A process in this direction has, in fact, already started; examples are the opt-outs and derogations granted to the United Kingdom and Denmark with regard to the Social Charter and EMU. But so far the process has been a defensive and disorganized reaction to the hesitation and unwillingness of some member states to go along with the others, and has sometimes taken place outside the EU framework and institutions, as in the case of the early EMS and the Schengen agreement. It would be unwise – and contrary to the whole history of European integration – to continue on this defensive course and let internal strife or public discontent dictate uncontrolled reform.

Successful reform requires non-trivial change in the constitutional structure of the Union, including significant revision of the Treaties and major modifications of European political institutions. It is true that such changes risk disturbing delicate balances: between the interests of different states and between national and supranational authority. Any proposed change requires careful consideration, since what happens in one field usually affects other fields as well.

The *status quo*, however, is no longer an option. The 1996 IGC is the natural starting point for change: it should respond to the challenges that confront Europe by producing economic, political and legal reforms of the European Union.

The aim of this Report is to inform the debate that must necessarily precede such reforms. Our premise is that a successful IGC must aim for comprehensive reform. It is important to consider reform as a simultaneous package, rather than as a set of unconnected marginal changes to the present structure of the Union. Positive interactions between different aspects of reform will, in fact, be a recurring theme. For instance, coming to grips with lax enforcement of the Single Market is much easier if the legitimacy problems of the Union's institutions are dealt with at the same time.

To avoid misunderstanding, let us emphasize that we do not wish to propose redrafting, from scratch, a new 'Constitution for Europe'. Instead we are deliberately eclectic. As our starting points, we take the four challenges discussed above and the process we already see in motion to modify European integration in the wake of these challenges. Nor do we intend our discussion to be exhaustive. We use a number of examples and cases to illustrate the basic arguments. Given that our comparative advantage lies mainly in economics, we focus on the policy areas within the first pillar of the EU according to the Maastricht Treaty.

1.3   Flexible integration

We have argued that the major challenges facing the Union are to make it fit for enlargement; to accommodate the different views on the appropriate scope and depth of European integration; and to close the democratic deficit to revive public support for the Union. The principal task of reform should be to accommodate the different demands of heterogeneous European interests by introducing more flexibility without risking the gains achieved through previous integration efforts. We suggest that the key to solving this difficult task is to make a distinction between, on the one hand, what all members consider to be essential about the

Union and, on the other hand, additional layers of integration on which there is no unanimity. A dual structure can be envisaged which includes:

- A *common base*, in which all members of the Union must participate, that encompasses a well-defined set of shared competences deemed essential to preserve the gains from free trade and mobility in a European Union open to new members.

- A possibility to enter into *open partnerships* that allow groups of countries to integrate further along policy dimensions outside the common base, without obliging other member countries to follow their lead.

We label this structure flexible integration. The duality is indispensable. Together, the two strike a proper balance between, one the one hand, a firm commitment of all states to the fundamental values of European integration and, on the other hand, freedom of choice both for those who wish to pursue deeper and broader integration and for those who do not. Flexible integration strengthens the effectiveness and legitimacy of the Union in its essential elements – the common base – and recognizes the greater heterogeneity of its members by separating these essentials from the optional elements of integration – the open partnerships.

This Report explores the requirements and implications of a European Union built around flexible integration. We discuss the principles underlying flexible integration and compare it with other ideas and proposals for reforming the European Union. No model of reform can be a panacea, of course, given the many issues involved. Flexible integration, too, has its potential problems and risks. We acknowledge these, but we also suggest ways to deal with them. These issues are dealt with more comprehensively in Chapters 3 and 4.

The most vital element of flexible integration is a definition of the common base accepted by all members. A relatively narrow definition is probably easier to agree upon, given the heterogeneous preferences in Europe regarding the scope of integration. It would also facilitate enlargement. A narrow definition of the common base, however, is not an essential characteristic of flexible integration. Furthermore, flexible integration allows addition to the common base of integration projects that began within open partnerships, provided that all members of the Union agree. Flexible integration is thus not a static concept, nor is it an obstacle to deeper and wider integration of the Union as a whole.

Given the Union's current structure and the challenges posed by enlargement, a natural starting point for the common base is the Single Market. The common base would then incorporate those elements of European integration necessary to preserve the four freedoms, namely a prohibition on barriers within the Union to mobility of goods, services, people and capital. In addition, the common base would include transfer programmes to make the Single Market politically viable. So far these have been the CAP and the Structural Funds. But the opportunity to make the transfer programmes more efficient should be exploited now, given the challenge that enlargement represents for the CAP and the Structural Funds. The importance of capital mobility also calls for including capital tax harmonization in the common base.

Today the Social Charter seems too controversial among the member states to make it a part of the common base. Similarly, the benefits of a single European money are debatable enough and the unwillingness of some states to give up their monetary sovereignty is strong enough to argue that a currency union fits better among the open partnerships than in the common base. Moreover, the Maastricht Treaty already granted some states the possibility to opt out of the single currency. Making the currency union an open partnership leaves the countries that wish to go ahead with a common currency early the option to do so under the timetable and provisions agreed in Maastricht without forcing others to do the same. A properly functioning Single Market, however, requires some coordination of macroeconomic policies. This suggests that the remaining provisions of stages II and III of EMU, that is macroeconomic surveillance, commitment to fiscal stability and central bank independence, should be part of the common base together with a practical strategy for monetary policy coordination to avoid competitive devaluations.

Depending on the pattern of international spillover effects, any particular policy area outside the common base might hold single or multiple open partnerships. To avoid friction between the open partnerships and the base, and between open partnerships concerned with different policy spheres, rules are needed for the formation of new partnerships. Responsibilities would have to be assigned to specific EU bodies for monitoring the proper working of the common base and for ensuring that it was not compromised by the activities of the open partnerships.

A central idea behind flexible integration is that the commitment to the cooperative agreements included in the common base would be stronger than it is today. Narrowing the common base to a well-defined set of competences makes it easier for the member states to accept transferring more sovereignty to the EU for the common administration of these competences. As we discuss at length in later chapters, this would allow stronger enforcement of Single Market legislation and a reduction of the democratic deficit.

Flexible integration incorporates a generalized principle of subsidiarity. As noted above, one source of tension in the Union today is that member states wishing to widen the scope of cooperation feel that they are being held back by other members. The generalized principle of subsidiarity leaves the decision to set up new forms of cooperation with the states that wish to do so, provided other members are not hurt and the rules of the Union are followed.

One advantage of the principle is that it allows for learning by doing: the Union as a whole can learn from the experience of a subgroup. Importantly, the open partnerships allow member states to reverse a new integration project at significantly lower cost. When the expected gains from integration are highly uncertain, this option is likely to encourage more experiments with new forms of integration. The learning and demonstration effects from such experimentation will promote the development of the Union as a whole.

There is another reason why open partnerships may, in practice, lead to deeper integration of the Union. It is often better to join a group than to be left out, even if the preferred outcome would have been to have no group at all. The European currency union may serve as an example. It is one thing to dislike a common European currency, as compared with a *status quo* of 14 or more national currencies; it is quite another thing to stay out of the currency union if all or most of the other members of the Union join. Thus creating the possibility for a group of states to form a currency union as an open partnership alters the pattern of incentives and may induce the rest of the Union to participate.

Flexible integration departs from one important rule of the existing European Union: to have, for each sphere of European integration, only one set of cooperative arrangements for all member states. The problem is that this set can only be the smallest common denominator among countries. This creates not only inflexibility but also a strong tension between deepening integration and enlarging the Union. The larger the Union, the smaller the set of arrangements on which all are willing to agree, and the larger the dissatisfaction for those states which favour more integration. An imperfect way to relieve this tension is the current practice of multispeed integration, where all states subscribe to the same set of European policies, but are allowed different deadlines for implementing them. Flexible integration explicitly recognizes the preference of some countries to share fewer competences inside the European Union.

Contrary to the vision of a United States of Europe, flexible integration thus recognizes the desire of some countries to limit the scope and depth of integration without preventing others from finding new and deeper forms of cooperation. Flexible integration also avoids the danger of a Europe *à la carte*, because all states are committed to the common base of shared competences in which all members of the Union must participate. This is absolutely essential in order to preserve the gains from cooperation.

Although flexible integration allows countries to integrate at different speeds over different dimensions, it does not – in contrast to the various proposals for variable geometry – imply a hard core of more integrated states and a periphery of those less integrated. The hierarchy implied by variable geometry risks creating a geographical schism between first-class and second-class European citizens. In contrast, flexible integration emphasizes a functional set of mandatory competences – the common base – and permits additional voluntary cooperative arrangements – the open partnerships. Even though states that want deeper integration are likely to participate in a larger number of partnerships, there is not necessarily a stigma attached to other states of being laggards, or second-class Europeans.

This is not to say that the option of creating open partnerships can never be divisive. This is a real possibility, particularly in areas of integration that entail strong policy spillovers between countries. The examples in Chapter 3 illustrate how divisiveness can arise. To handle such risks, we argue that countries choosing not to participate in the formation of open partnerships should nevertheless have a say in their formation, and that in turn they can be required to follow *rules of good conduct*. Our proposal for monetary cooperation is a concrete example.

One response to this Report may be to insist that flexible forms of integration already exist in Europe today, in the genesis of the European Monetary System, or in the Schengen agreement to abolish internal border controls. Why reform the Union, if flexible partnerships can already be formed outside the formal framework of European integration?

The answer has three important dimensions. First, cooperation outside the Union may interfere with the proper functioning of the Union itself, undermining its basic elements of free trade and mobility. An example would be projects of industrial policy that would re-erect non-tariff trade barriers around a subgroup of Union members. Bringing such activities into the framework of the Union allows easier monitoring and provides a structured forum for resolving conflicts between member states. Second, cooperation outside the European Union – particularly a larger Union than today's – may create exclusive groups that could become politically divisive. An example would be a monetary union formed by the Northern European states alone, with no real prospect of entry for the other members of the Union. Third, with growing Union membership, outside cooperative arrangements might start to mushroom. This would make it more and more difficult for European citizens to understand the identity of the European Union. Ultimately, this could only contribute to rising public dissatisfaction with the Union.

1.4   Institutional reform

The idea of a European Union based on flexible integration raises many questions. It also points naturally towards specific directions for reform in dealing with the Union's current problems. In this section we give a brief overview of some of the answers suggested by the discussion in Chapters 5–7 of the Report.

1.4.1   A transparent legal order

The dual structure of flexible integration can be used directly in constitutional reform of the EU. It naturally suggests a legal hierarchy, with the basic principles of EU governance, including the definition of the common base, enshrined in a Treaty on European Union (Union Treaty) with constitutional status. Most of the substantive rules needed to give effect to the common policies, however, could be incorporated in a lower level of law. The latter would thus become more flexible and adaptable to changing circumstances. The Union Treaty would also contain the general rules for setting up and changing open partnerships, including rules for entry and exit. The substantive rules relating to individual open partnerships, however, would be determined by specific agreements between the participating countries.

1.4.2   Serious enforcement of the common policies

Two principles should govern reform to improve enforcement in the Single Market. First, the European Commission should not have sole responsibility for enforcement. Today the Commission has many contradictory missions that create conflicts of interests and weaken its enforcement powers. Enforcement should, therefore, be delegated to new and specialized bodies, for example, an independent European competition agency. These bodies and the Commission would together have the responsibility for enforcement. One possibility, discussed in the Report, is to give the agency a clear mission to act as an 'advocate' for the unorganized European consumer; this would balance the well-defined interests of, say, two companies proposing to merge or a member state proposing to give a subsidy. The decision would stay with the Commission, which would be the 'judge' arbitrating between the two sides of the argument.

Second, measures are needed to strengthen individual citizens' legal rights of action against violations of Union law, including the possibility of taking EU bodies and national governments to court. A concrete measure would be to institute a European circuit court meeting regularly in different places throughout the Union. To facilitate such action, and to increase transparency generally, more open procedures would be required, such that information from the political and administrative bodies of the EU becomes more accessible to the citizens and the media. These kinds of reforms would promote the enforcement of the Single Market from below, by individual citizens.

Official jargon notwithstanding, it is an implicitly recognized fact that some member states are less committed than others to enforcing the four freedoms of the Single Market. This tacit understanding goes hand in hand with laxer enforcement of all Union legislation in the less committed countries. Lax enforcement, however, tends to spill over to any country which feels that a particular measure hurts its interests. If mandatory integration is limited to the areas in the common base, it becomes more realistic to insist on serious enforcement.

1.4.3   Efficient and legitimate decision-making

To improve efficiency and to avoid outright gridlock after enlargement it will be necessary to move away from unanimity to majority rule in Union decision-making. One advantage of anchoring the Union to a clearly defined common base is that the common policies can be integrated more deeply without raising fears that supranationalism would automatically spread to other, more contentious, policy areas. Within a narrow set of competences – the Single Market and related policies – flexible integration thus allows for genuinely supranational decisions at the European level. This does not mean that the European Union would become a federal state. Unlike a state, the Union would have no authority to expand its own competences beyond the common base as defined in the Treaty. Expansion of the common base would require a Treaty revision and thus need the unanimous agreement of all member states; and unwarranted proposals by EU bodies, surpassing the limits of the common base, would be subject to review by an appropriate judicial body. The logic for supranationalism is that states which voluntarily have transferred certain competences to the European level would also accept to delegate the management of those competences to European bodies.

For such delegation to become acceptable, secure delimitation of the common base is not enough; the supranational European bodies also need a high degree of democratic legitimacy in the public eye (a similar point can be made about serious enforcement). Legitimacy, in turn, requires that a range of interests are represented, protected and well balanced against each other. It also requires that decision-makers can be held accountable in a relatively direct way.

National interests in the Union are naturally, and strongly, represented in the Council. A reformed system of qualified majority voting, requiring votes to represent a majority of the EU population, in addition to the existing weighting system for states, could help balance the interests of big and small countries.

Cross-border interests are, however, very weakly represented in the current Union. The European Parliament is the natural place for such representation. To balance national and European-wide cross-border interests, the Union could apply majority decision-making in all areas of the common base, with a more equal sharing of powers between the Council and the Parliament. The Parliament's powers could also be extended to share the right to initiate legislation with the Commission. Appropriate electoral reform should, however, precede such changes in the power structure. Specifically, each citizen could be given two votes: one on a majority ballot for a local representative and one on a pan-European proportional ballot. The seats allocated by the first ballot would ensure representation of local interests in the Parliament, whereas those allocated by the second would encourage the formation of true cross-border political parties. Such parties would give more life to debates on European issues concerning all citizens of the Union and, thereby, build bridges between existing national opinions.

Greater control of the Commission could come about, for instance, by allowing the Parliament to approve or reject Council proposals for the appointment of individual Commissioners, not just the Commission as a whole.

After such reforms the governance of the common base – and of the common base alone – could gradually evolve towards a system of bicameral decision-making, with the European Parliament and the Council as the two chambers and the Commission as a still powerful, but more accountable, agenda setter.

1.4.4   Clear assignments of EU functions

The current structure of the Union lacks transparency, because supranational and intergovernmental integration are mixed up in the same EU bodies and because the division of responsibilities across these bodies is fuzzy. Flexible integration would contribute to greater transparency by separating the common policies in the supranational common base from the voluntary integration projects in the open partnerships, which, from the Union's perspective, are intergovernmental arrangements.

Another important aspect of institutional reform is to assign different policy-making functions to specific Union bodies. We present two possible reform scenarios below, which, although quite different, share the common feature of defining more clearly the division of responsibility among the EU bodies governing the common policies. Clearer assignments would certainly create greater transparency, allow for better accountability and, it is hoped, produce better performance.

The two scenarios can be distinguished by their different assignments for the European Commission. In the first, the Commission would be responsible for the administration and enforcement of the common base, and for ensuring that open partnerships do not interfere with the base. It would also implement external economic policies related to the common base on behalf of the EU. Within this limited domain the Commission would be free to develop policy initiatives to safeguard the common base against new challenges as they arise. But it would not be allowed to venture outside the domain of the common base without a clear mandate from the member states.

In this scenario, reform of the Commission itself could be relatively limited; strengthening its accountability to the European Parliament and the European Council would help to close the current democratic deficit. The scenario would, however, leave the

Union without the Commission exercising political leadership in favour of the 'European cause'. Other political forces would have to develop to balance European interests against the national interests represented in the Council. After appropriate electoral reform, cross-border majorities within a stronger European Parliament may well – if European citizens so desire – take over as the driving force of European integration. In any case, limiting the Commission to a purely administrative function can only be envisaged if another powerful advocate for Europe emerges.

In the second scenario, the Commission would retain its current political leadership in promoting European integration in addition to administering the base. A Commission with a strong political mandate needs much more democratic legitimacy than it has now, however; we discuss alternative routes to making the Commission more accountable in the Report. Furthermore, a Commission with a mandate for political leadership would remain a politicized body, subject to the temptation to mingle its administrative functions with the building of political coalitions for new policy initiatives. It would, therefore, be particularly important to create a set of new and independent regulatory institutions. These would have significant administrative powers and be charged with executing policies in areas such as merger control or competition policy, where interest groups seek to exercise influence. In the first scenario, with the Commission limited to administration of the common base, delegation to such independent bodies would still be desirable, but less urgent.

1.4.5   Macroeconomic coordination and the single currency

Macroeconomic coordination to avoid temporary, tariff-like disruptions of the Single Market by competitive devaluations has always been at the centre of European integration. Such coordination should be part of the common base. Traditionally, the EU has relied on one or another form of fixed exchange rates: one of the first objectives written into the Treaty of Rome includes a reference to stable exchange rates. But with increasing capital mobility this coordination device has become more fragile, as witnessed by the recent turmoil in financial markets and the effective breakdown of the ERM. The central banks in a hard core of states continue to coordinate their monetary policies with

Germany and maintain their currencies in narrow ERM bands. But for another group of EU members this is neither a realistic nor a desirable option in the short run. How can coordination for these countries be achieved without the tarnished fixed exchange-rate mechanism? This is also a relevant question in the longer run: it is likely that some EU members will not want – or will not be allowed – to come along, if the single currency envisaged in the Maastricht Treaty becomes reality.

The solution we discuss in the Report is to require all EU members to adopt inflation targets. Progress towards achieving these targets would then be monitored by the institutions of the European System of Central Banks. The inflation targets need not be the same for all states. The common mechanism and prospective sanctions for apparent target violations, however, would make it more costly for countries to engineer competitive devaluations. Furthermore, inflation targets may help stabilize expectations and reduce financial instability without inviting speculative attacks, because exchange rates would no longer have to be fixed in narrow bands.

It is necessary to introduce more flexibility than is in the Maastricht Treaty with regard to European currency union. Something more than the mere coordination of monetary policy is at issue, namely the adoption of a common currency – the third stage of the current EMU project. Today such integration may be feasible, and perhaps desirable, among a few states, but certainly not among all.

Once it is agreed that some EU states can adopt a common currency as an open partnership, there is a key problem to address: how to coordinate monetary policy between the currency union and the rest of the EU. This fundamental problem was neglected by the Maastricht negotiations, because of the assumption that the currency union would eventually include all states. Flexible integration offers an obvious way to solve the policy coordination problem. If the rules of the common base require states to adopt inflation targets, the currency union would also be required to adopt such a target. The remaining problem is how to design the entry rules.

1.5   The second and third pillars of the EU

As stated in section 2, the Report focuses on the issues related to the first pillar of the EU according to the Maastricht Treaty: the European Community. But the general ideas we put forward can also be applied to the second and third pillars, of justice and home affairs, and of a common foreign and defence policy. The principles of flexible integration call for distinguishing, within the domain of these two pillars, between the basic principles of European Union enshrined in the common base and other areas where policy coordination is optional.

Commitment to democratic government and the rule of law as well as the observance of human rights should be central elements of the common base. Governments following or allowing undemocratic practices should thus risk losing the benefits of EU membership, which would raise the cost of political adventurism. Including these basic principles in the common base would also give citizens of new democracies an option to complain before EU institutions against political malfeasance in their home countries at a time when domestic institutions are still weak. Tying EU membership firmly and visibly to these basic principles would thus help secure and develop the new democracies in Eastern and Central Europe that are now candidates for membership.

Mutual assurance of non-aggression also seems to be a natural element of the common base. This would imply that members cannot enter different alliances with non-members that might oppose each other. Beyond that, national interests in foreign and defence policy – and indeed national ways and traditions of thinking about these issues – are, at present, too diverse realistically to make a common EU foreign and defence policy part of the common base.

In defence, there is certainly room for open partnerships, accommodating more limited cooperation, such as the joint Franco-German military corps. Also, member states that pursue common foreign policy interests *vis-à-vis* outsiders might well do so in an open partnership, provided this interest does not conflict with the stated interests of other members or of the Union as a whole. This would have the advantage of the open partnership being clearly recognized as a subgroup of the EU. Its initiatives would thus not be mistaken as initiatives of the Union itself and would not commit, directly nor indirectly, other member states against their wishes. Open partnerships can also be imagined in the area of home affairs. A case in point may be the coordination of anti-drug efforts by national police forces, as the benefits from such coordination tend primarily to be shared by neighbouring states.

1.6   Structure of the Report

The Report is organized as follows. In Chapter 2 we briefly survey the history and the institutional development of European integration since 1945 to understand the reasons for success in previous decades and the reasons why current institutions are ill-suited to face the challenges of the future. Chapter 3 examines flexible integration in more detail, explaining why it produces a mix of commitment and flexibility that is superior both to the *status quo* and to other proposals for reform, and illustrating how it may work with the help of some simplified examples. Chapter 4 discusses which economic policies should be in the common base, starting from the premise that it should contain the policies necessary to make the Single Market economically efficient and politically viable. Chapter 5 looks at how to improve enforcement of EU law in the common base. Chapter 6 discusses the formation of open partnerships, with particular attention to European currency union. Finally, Chapter 7 specifies possible avenues for reform of the EU political institutions, so as to reduce the democratic deficit and enhance the accountability of EU bodies to the citizens of Europe.

2   European integration, 1945–95

2.1   Origins and growth of the European Union

Europe has changed dramatically over the past 50 years. The second world war shattered the economies of all the European states. In many countries the legitimacy of the nation states was brought into question by the economic and political failures that led up to the war and by military defeat and occupation. Immediately after the war the continent was divided into two politico-military blocs separated by the iron curtain.

Post-war European integration started in 1948 with the formation of the Organisation for European Economic Cooperation (OEEC) organized around the United States. Initially created to administer the Marshall Plan, it played an important role in facilitating intra-European trade during the post-war reconstruction. In the mid-1950s some OEEC members moved to greater economic cooperation. The initial approach was in sectors that were particularly sensitive both economically and politically. The European Coal and Steel Community (ECSC) addressed the ruinous competition resulting from excess capacity in coal and steel; it also brought the industries at the heart of states' capacities to make war under shared authority. Euratom later tackled the sensitive market for nuclear energy.

The European Economic Community (EEC), created in 1958, represented a much broader move towards European integration. It started as a customs union with a common external tariff and a number of common policies, particularly for agriculture, but was destined to become a common market within a decade.

The six founding nations of these three Communities – Belgium, France, Germany, Italy, Luxembourg and the Netherlands – expressed clear political ambitions. The preamble to the 1957 Treaty of Rome stated their determination 'to lay the foundations of an ever closer union among the peoples of Europe ... [in order] to preserve and strengthen peace and liberty'. Article 2 of the Treaty defined the task of the EEC as being 'to promote throughout the Community a harmonious development of economic activities, a continuous and balanced expansion, an increase in stability, an accelerated raising of the standard of living and closer relations between the States belonging to it'. This required 'establishing a common market and progressively approximating the economic policies of Member States'. Securing peace and liberty through political integration and increasing prosperity through economic integration were regarded as interdependent objectives of the Community.

Responding to the establishment of the EEC, Austria, Denmark, Norway, Portugal, Sweden, Switzerland and the UK formed the European Free Trade Association (EFTA) in 1960, a much looser arrangement than the EEC. EFTA was later joined by Finland and Iceland. The EEC, however, quickly emerged as the more dynamic form of economic integration and became a magnet for other European states. No country has left the Community since its creation. On the contrary, it has attracted six of the nine EFTA members in addition to Greece, Ireland and Spain, and has received membership applications from another half-dozen states, including several from the now defunct COMECON. The success of the Community made it plausible to claim that: 'Confusion between "Europe" and the "European Community" may ... gradually resolve itself in a progressive identity between the two' (Gerbet, 1994).

The late 1970s and early 1980s were periods of stagnation in European integration, marked by growing dissatisfaction with the Community's inability to solve its internal problems and growing awareness of the fact that the common market was undermined by non-tariff barriers to trade, such as national differences in product and safety regulations and rules for public procurement. The process of integration was finally revived by the Single European Act (SEA) of 1986, which strengthened the Community's decision-making powers and launched a programme aiming at the completion of the Single European Market for goods, services, capital and labour. This revival culminated in the Treaty on European Union adopted in Maastricht in 1992.

2.2 Expansion in trade, transfers and decision-making

Perhaps the simplest way to summarize the development of economic integration over the past 47 years is to look at the *four freedoms*: the mobility of goods, services, labour and capital. We can gauge the impact of the EEC by looking at the extent to which economic activity remains centred on individual states, how far it involves partners in the EC, and how far it involves trade with the rest of the world. Progress in European integration should be marked by a rising share of intra-EC activity. Table 2.1 gives the answers.

The markets for goods have integrated remarkably, the share of intra-EC trade in GDP having nearly tripled between 1960 and 1990, while the share of extra-EC trade increased by only a third. In contrast, integration in the markets for services was still fairly modest by 1990, although it is now rising, particularly in the area of financial services. Between 1960 and 1970 the share of extra-Community foreign workers in the EC labour force rose from 1% to 3%. However, despite long-standing legal guarantees of internal mobility of labour, migration between EC member countries has remained small.

Assessing capital mobility is more complicated. Table 2.1 shows that, by 1990, internal foreign direct investment had remained negligible. With the removal of practically all capital controls in the course of the Single Market programme, however, EC financial markets are now almost perfectly integrated as demonstrated by the disappearance of spreads between offshore and onshore interest rates and the speed and volume of capital flows that shook the European Monetary System in 1992 and 1993. Thus, when the Maastricht Treaty was negotiated in 1991, the Single Market was largely a reality for goods and financial investments, and increasingly so for services.

Table 2.1 The four freedoms of the European internal market, 1960–90

		1960	*1970*	*1980*	*1990*
Goods	Intra	6	8	13	17
(trade as % of GDP)	Extra	9	10	11	12
Services	Intra	–	–	3	3
(trade as % of GDP)	Extra	–	–	2	3
Labour	Intra	2	2	2	2
(foreigners as % of labour force)	Extra	1	3	3	3
Capital					
FDI	Intra	–	1	1	2
(FDI as % of domestic investment)	Extra	–	1	2	2
Investment income	Intra	–	–	1	2
(income as % of GDP)	Extra	–	1	2	3

Source: Molle (1994)

As intra-Community trade expands, we should expect a corresponding growth in the numbers of decision-makers regulating the Single Market, of groups seeking to influence their decisions and of disputes involving the Community's legal framework. These developments are reflected by the indicators in Table 2.2. The Commission's staff steadily increased to 17,000 employees in 1990. However, it remains small in comparison with the 8 million civil servants employed by the 12 member states in 1994. The importance of EC institutions is probably better gauged by the explosion (from 400 to 3,000 between 1980 and 1990) in the number of lobbying organizations listed in the Commission's *Directory of EC Trade and Professional Associations*, a sure sign of the prominence EC institutions have gained. Another indicator is the number of judgements pronounced by the European Court of Justice, which multiplied sevenfold between 1970 and 1990.

Table 2.2 Evolution of European institutions, 1960–90

	1960	*1970*	*1980*	*1990*
Permanent Commission civil servants (thousands)	1	5	11	17
Number of EC lobby organizations	167	309	410	3,000
Number of judgements pronounced by the European Court of Justice	–	240	830	1,780

Source: Molle (1994)

The Community budget is a further indicator of European integration. The EC general budget rose from 0.54% of EC–6 GDP in 1975 to 1.28% of EC–12 GDP in 1994. But it still remains modest in comparison with the member states' national budgets: in 1994 the EC budget amounted to only 2.5% of the combined budgets of the member states. Two items completely dominate the budgetary expenditure of the EC: the Common Agricultural Policy – roughly 50% of the 1994 budget – and the structural and cohesion funds – about 30% of the 1994 budget.

In conclusion, real but somewhat slow progress has been achieved towards the objective of economic integration. Goods markets were substantially integrated by 1990, and barriers to the free mobility of services, labour and capital are disappearing as a result of the 1992 Single Market programme. Limited as it is, growth in the EC budget indicates that the member states have been willing to develop systems of transnational transfer payments.[1] Such systems can help improve the economic efficiency of the Single Market, yet their existence reflects a political as much as an economic rationale: transfer programmes were often necessary to overcome the resistance of interest groups to European integration.

Economic integration has also promoted better economic performance by raising capital accumulation and technological progress, thus increasing EC economic growth. Although the mechanics are relatively easy to describe in theory, the effects of integration on growth are more difficult to measure precisely. The relatively small number of empirical studies that have been conducted find a positive impact of EC integration on GDP growth of between 0.2 and 0.5 percentage points per annum.[2] Furthermore, economic integration has fostered the convergence of the EC economies. Recent empirical studies suggest that the speed of convergence of the relatively poorer countries to the richer countries was faster during the 1960s and 1970s inside the EC than among non-participating countries (Walz, 1995).

On the political front, the essential purpose of the Community has been achieved. War between France, Germany, Italy and the United Kingdom is now unthinkable. Increasing prosperity, to which the Community contributed, has made social tensions more manageable. The Community has also helped build and consolidate a consensus in Europe about fundamental constitutional principles: the rule of law, democracy and respect for individual rights. Somewhat paradoxically, it is the nation states rather than the Community that have enjoyed the largest gains of legitimacy owing to these political achievements.

2.3 The institutional framework of integration

The Common Market together with the common policies formed the core of the original EEC. The Common Market aimed at the elimination of obstacles to free mobility of goods, services, labour and capital. The common policies were to cover four areas: commercial policy, agriculture, transport and competition. In these areas the member states were supposed to transfer decision-making powers to the Community, granting it the authority to formulate and carry out its own policies. While the Treaty of Rome called for coordination of monetary and fiscal policies, this was effectively supplied externally by the Bretton Woods system. Common policies for trade, agriculture and competition were established in the 1960s but, until the mid-1980s, the main obstacles to free trade had been removed only in the goods markets.[3]

The success of economic integration depends importantly on decisions taken by the relevant political bodies. The EU's institutional development is unique. Unlike any other group of countries, the EU has vested itself with institutions whose nature and mandate transcend the intergovernmental character of coventional international organizations. In this section we review the development of these institutions from the creation of the EEC in 1958 to the foundation of the European Union in 1993, when the Maastricht Treaty came into effect.

2.3.1 Community institutions

The main institutions of the Community are the Commission, the Council of Ministers, the European Parliament and the Court of Justice.[4] There is also the European Council, which has a broad political mandate in relation to the Union.

The Commission

The Commission is a supranational body. Its members, the Commissioners, are mandated individually and collectively to perform as advocates of the Community interest. They are independent from the national governments in the sense that they must not, under oath, seek or take instructions from them or from any other outside body. The Commission is appointed by common accord of the member governments and the approval of the European Parliament. Although there is at least one Commissioner per member state and Commissioners are nominated by individual member governments, governments cannot recall them after their appointment. In practice, however, Commissioners sometimes act as advocates of national interests.

The Commission is appointed for terms of four years. There are currently 20 Commissioners, two each from the larger member states – France, Germany, Italy, Spain and the United Kingdom – and one from each of the remaining countries. The President of the Commission and the two Vice-Presidents are chosen from among the Commissioners. Their appointments are for renewable two-year terms. There is no formal rule for how to propose a president; in practice, the European Council makes that decision. The Commission constitutes and acts as a college. Where voting is necessary, it decides by simple majority. The president is a *primus inter pares* with his colleagues and enjoys no special decision-making powers.

As the guardian of the European Treaties, the Commission is the watchdog of the correct implementation of Community law and policies. Under Article 169 of the Treaty on European Union, the Commission can take legal action against member governments on these matters, and frequently does so. Moreover, the Commission makes decisions that are binding on private parties and which private parties can challenge in the European Court of First Instance. In its executive duties, the Commission's role is to implement decisions taken by the Council of Ministers. In its function of promoting European integration the Commission has the mandate to develop new initiatives in the areas of the Treaty.

The Council

Proposals made by the Commission are submitted to the Council of Ministers, the main legislative body in most areas covered by the Treaties. It consists of representatives of the member states at ministerial level, whose unambiguous role is to represent national interests. The Council meets in different compositions according to the policy issues tackled; agriculture ministers for CAP discussions, trade ministers for trade matters, and so on. The General Affairs Council (consisting of foreign ministers) plays something of a coordinating role. The Council presidency rotates among the EU member governments in terms of six months each, a feature that prevents countries from gaining strong leadership or a hegemonic role.

As a legislative body, the Council is distinct from national legislatures in two key respects. First, it is not directly elected. States are represented on the Council by agents of national (or occasionally regional) *governments*. Second, decisions require unanimity unless the Treaty provides for qualified majority voting. Even where the Treaty does provide for majority voting, a state can invoke the *Luxembourg compromise* of 1966, which was interpreted in practice as giving each member state the power to veto any decision where very important national interests are at stake. Significantly, the compromise provides no criteria to evaluate the notion of 'very important interests'. Thus no state has to accept a decision that it strongly dislikes.[5] These two characteristics make the Council an intergovernmental body.

Under majority voting, each state is assigned a number of votes on the Council. Before the latest enlargement, the number of votes was 10 each for France, Germany, Italy and the United Kingdom, 8 for Spain, 5 each for Belgium, Greece, the Netherlands and Portugal, 3 each for Denmark and Ireland, and 2 for Luxembourg: a total of 76. A qualified majority required 54 votes, while a decision could be blocked with 23 votes. This distribution gives the smaller states a larger weight on the Council than if votes were distributed according to population size. Scaling the total number such that Luxembourg would obtain one vote, 1991 population figures would imply 176 votes for Germany, 127 each for the United Kingdom and Italy, 125 for France, 86 for Spain, 33 for the Netherlands, 22 each for Belgium, Greece and Portugal, 11 for Denmark and 8 for Ireland (see Table 2.3).

Austria and Sweden received four votes each upon entry to the Union, while Finland received three. Since the most recent enlargement, a qualified majority requires 62 votes and a blocking minority 26. Yielding to the pressure of the United Kingdom, the Council committed itself in the *Ioannina compromise* of 30 March 1994 to 'make every effort to find a satisfactory solution that can be adopted by at least 68 votes within a reasonable time', when 23 to 26 votes are cast against a proposal.

In sum, Council decisions implicitly favour the smaller members of the Union. Interestingly, the Council rules of procedure now provide that any Council member or a Commissioner can propose to vote on an issue. There is then a procedural vote. If a simple majority is in favour of voting on the substantive issue, then a vote is taken. This means that the strength of both the Luxembourg and the Ioannina compromises depends on enough states being willing to subordinate their preferences on a particular issue to the principle of maintaining the compromises.

Summit meetings of heads of state or government of the member states have taken place regularly since 1974. These meetings developed into the 'European Council', which took on the task of giving political leadership to the Community, although its role had no specific basis in the Treaties at the time. The European Council eventually received formal recognition in the SEA, which also provided for the President of the Commission to attend its meetings. The Maastricht Treaty says that the European Council is to supply the impetus and political guidelines necessary for the further development of the Union.

Table 2.3 Weights of member states in European institutions

Member state	Population (thousands)	Votes in the Council	Seats in the Parliament	Commissioners
Belgium	10,050	5	25	1
Denmark	5,190	3	16	1
Germany	81,190	10	99	2
Greece	10,350	5	25	1
Spain	39,140	8	64	2
France	57,660	10	87	2
Ireland	3,560	3	15	1
Italy	57,070	10	87	2
Luxembourg	280	2	6	1
Netherlands	15,300	5	31	1
Portugal	9,860	5	25	1
United Kingdom	57,920	10	87	2
Austria	7,867	4	21	1
Finland	5,080	3	16	1
Sweden	8,750	4	22	1
Total	369,267	87	626	20

The European Parliament

Since 1979 the members of the European Parliament (EP) have been directly elected for terms of four years. Their mandate is to represent 'the peoples of the States', not a common EU electorate. The EP is, therefore, not fully supranational, despite the fact that most parliamentary decisions are made by majority vote.[6]

The EP has a total of 626 members, 99 from Germany, 87 each from France, the United Kingdom and Italy, 64 from Spain, 31 from the Netherlands, 25 each from Belgium, Greece and Portugal, 22 from Sweden, 21 from Austria, 16 each from Denmark and Finland, 15 from Ireland and 6 from Luxembourg. As in the Council, the smaller states are relatively overrepresented in the Parliament (see Table 2.3).

There are no political parties overarching national borders. Parliamentarians with similar political positions form *political groups* to work together. The minimum number of parliamentarians needed to form a political group is 29 if they come from the same member state, 23 if they come from two, 18 if they come from three, and 14 if they come from four or more member states. There are currently nine such groups plus some *non-attached* members.

The EP works in over 20 committees. Chairmanships of the committees are determined by the political groups according to a proportional formula based on their size. Apart from the chairmanship, being a *rapporteur* on a particular piece of business is an influential position that is also in the gift of the political groups.

The Court of Justice and the Court of First Instance
The Court of Justice is the highest authority on the correct interpretation and application of Community law. Its 15 judges are each appointed for a term of six years. They act completely independently of governments. There is no requirement in the Treaties that there should be one judge from each country, although this has been the practice in the past. No dissenting or minority judgements are published and Court deliberations are held in secret. These practices have helped the Court to remain independent.

It has also played an active role in promoting European integration. In the 1960s the Court of Justice developed the idea of the supremacy of Community law over national law as one of the fundamental principles of the Community's architecture, stating that: 'By creating a Community of unlimited duration, having its own institutions, its own legal capacity and capacity of representation on the international plane and, more particularly, real powers stemming from a limitation of sovereignty or a transfer of powers from the States to the Community, the Member States have limited their sovereign rights, albeit within limited fields, and thus have created a body of law which binds both their nationals and themselves'.[7]

In its landmark *Cassis de Dijon* ruling of 1979,[8] the Court invented the principle of mutual recognition, which became an essential aspect of the Commission's effort to complete the internal market by 1992. More generally, the Court has emphasized the duty of national courts to apply Community law and to give it precedence over national law in case of conflict. It has also developed Community law as a source of legal rights and duties for individuals enforceable in national courts.

The Court of First Instance was created by the Single European Act. By relieving the Court of Justice from the burden of hearing all legal challenges, the role of the Court of First Instance is to increase the judicial capacity of the European Community.

Decision-making procedures

Current procedures for decision-making in the European Union are the consultation procedure, the cooperation procedure, the co-decision procedure and the conformity vote (see Table 2.4). Under all four, the Commission has the monopoly right of initiative and is responsible for drafting proposals as well as redrafting proposals amended or rejected by Parliament. The Commission's agenda-setting power is attenuated by the Council's right to amend proposals from the Commission, although, in the co-decision and the cooperation procedures, the Council can do so only by unanimity. Moreover, the Council can ask the Commission to draft proposals. If the European Parliament rejects a proposal under the co-decision procedure, a conciliation committee with equal representation of the European Parliament and the Council is formed to modify the Commission's proposal.

Table 2.4 indicates that the power of European Parliament differs significantly under the three procedures. Under the consultation procedure, the Parliament's role is reduced to giving an opinion. Under the cooperation procedure, the Parliament's decision determines the voting procedure (unanimity versus qualified majority) on the Council. If the Parliament decides to amend a proposal from the Commission and the latter accepts the amendment, the Council can amend this proposal only by unanimity, whereas it can adopt it by qualified majority. The Parliament's rejection of a proposal can be overruled by unanimous vote in the Council. Finally, under the co-decision procedure, Parliament and Council work together to find a compromise in the case of disagreement over a proposal from the Commission. This implies that the Parliament can now veto proposals under this

Table 2.4 Current decision-making procedures

1. Consultation procedure

- The Commission proposes
- The European Parliament gives an opinion
- The Council votes:

(a) with qualified majority
- derogation in competition policy (TEU 84)
- state aids (TEU 100c)
- visas starting in 1996 (TEU 106(6))
- provisions for statutes of ECB (TEU 109f(6))
- draft legislation within competence of EMI (TEU 109j(3))
- decision on entry in stage III of EMU (TEU 125)
- implementing decisions relative to European Social Fund
- research and development policies not mentioned elsewhere (TEU 130y)
- agreements with third countries

(b) with unanimity
- right to vote and be candidate in municipal and local elections (TEU 8b)
- reduction of customs rights (TEU 14)
- freedom of establishment (TEU 54)
- derogations to transport policy (TEU 75)
- harmonization of indirect taxation (TEU 99)
- common market (TEU 100)
- revision of rules concerning excessive deficits (TEU 104c)
- ECU exchange rate policies towards other currencies (TEU 109(1))
- appointment of executive board of ECB (TEU 109a(2))
- appointment of President of EMI (TEU 109f(1))
- stage III of EMU (TEU 109f(7))
- Article 2(3) of social chapter
- industry (specific measures) (TEU 130)
- specific actions on Economic and Social Cohesion (TEU 130b)
- nomination of President of Commission (TEU 158)
- financial provisions (own resources) (TEU 201)
- budgetary implementation (TEU 209)
- conclusion of international Treaties (TEU 208)

2. Cooperation procedure (instituted by SEA)

- The Commission proposes
- If the EP accepts, then the Council votes with qualified majority
- If the EP refuses, then Council votes with unanimity

Applies to:

- common rules of transport (TEU 75)
- rail, road and inland waterways (TEU 84)
- detailed rules of multilateral surveillance of economic policy (TEU 103(5))
- definitions for prohibition of privileged access and credit by ECB (TEU 104 a and b)
- measures to harmonize coinage (TEU 105a)
- minimum requirements for health and safety (TEU 118a)
- vocational training policy (TEU 127)
- implementation of decisions on European Social Fund and European Regional Development Fund (TEU 125 and 130e)
- implementation of multi-annual framework programmes on R&D (TEU 130o)
- basic objectives of environment (TEU 130s(1))
- development cooperation (TEU 130w)

3. Co-decision procedure (instituted by TEU)

- The Commission proposes

- If the EP accepts, the Council votes with qualified majority

- If the EP refuses, a conciliation committee is formed between EP and Council members. An amended proposal needs the vote of both the EP and Council with qualified majority

Applies to:

- generally the free movement of persons, services and capital except for Article 14 and 54 (TEU 49, 54, 56 and 57)
- internal market (TEU 100a)
- education, vocational training and youth (TEU 126)
- culture (unanimity in the Council) (TEU 128)
- public health (TEU 129)
- consumer protection (TEU 129a)
- trans-European networks (TEU 129d)
- R&D framework programme (unanimity in the Council) (TEU 130 I(1))
- environment programmes and priority objectives (TEU 130s(3))

4. Conformity vote

- The Commission proposes

- If the EP refuses, the proposal is rejected

- If the EP accepts, the Council must vote unanimously

Applies to:

- accession of new members
- international association agreements

procedure. The same is true under the conformity vote. In this case a proposal must be accepted by the Parliament and, with unanimity, by the Council in order to pass.

Community acts passed under the consultation, the cooperation or the co-decision procedures are either *directives* or *regulations*. A regulation is binding and directly applicable in all member states. A directive is binding as regards the results to be achieved, but allows the member states the choice of how to implement it.

In addition to these acts there are *decisions*, which are directed at individuals or member states and which are made by the Council or the Commission in their own right according to the relevant provision of the Treaty.[9]

2.3.2 Missing institutional structures: Enforcement and flexibility

It is also important to note what the European institutional framework does not contain in comparison to national political institutions. Of critical importance is the absence of Community-level mechanisms for implementing and enforcing Community law. The Commission is an executive without administrative functions reaching into the member states and without a police force. It must, therefore, rely on national governments not only to implement directives but also to punish recalcitrants, even in cases where the Court of Justice has ruled. Implementation and enforcement are thus profoundly intergovernmental. Also important is the limited use of delegated decision-making and standard-setting; competition policy being an important exception. The Council and the Parliament do not, for example, pass legislation giving fairly broad outlines of product safety standards and then delegate specific standard-setting authority to the Commission or an agency. Instead the Commission proposes detailed standards which are then legislated into inflexible directives and regulations.

The existing institutional arrangements have had critical effects on economic integration. In particular, the use of the unanimity rule in the Council before 1986 came at a high cost in terms of the flexibility and adaptability of decisions. The more extensive use of qualified majorities instituted by the SEA was crucial to complete the internal market. On the other hand, the full benefits of decisions taken since 1986 have not always been realized as a result of the lack of sufficient enforcement institutions.

2.3.3   European Union

Despite the enforcement problems, the Single Market programme was an enormous success for the Community. Jacques Delors, the President of the Commission, sought to build upon the success of the SEA and to maintain the momentum for deeper economic and political integration through the proposal for economic and monetary union (EMU) in 1989. The eventual result was the Maastricht Treaty, which instituted the European Union (EU).

The Union rests on three *pillars*. The first pillar consists of the three European Communities: ECSC, Euratom and the EEC (the latter now renamed officially the European Community – EC). The second and third pillars consist respectively of a common foreign and security policy (CFSP), and cooperation in the fields of justice and home affairs (JHA). These two pillars are designed to be basically intergovernmental in character, although there are provisions allowing the Council to decide to use majority voting for implementation of CFSP decisions and to bring some JHA matters into the first pillar.

The Maastricht Treaty expanded the scope of the EC by adding two blocks: economic and monetary union, including the 'third stage' of EMU (the irrevocable fixing of exchange parities between national currencies, followed by their replacement by a single European currency); and an agreement on social policy, going beyond the limited social policy provisions of the original Treaty as amended by the SEA.

The Treaty recognised the need for *commitment* to past accomplishments in calling for the maintenance of the *acquis communautaire*. Short of leaving the Union altogether, a member state cannot opt out of any part of the *acquis* and new member states must accept the *acquis* in full. The Treaty also introduced flexibility in the two new areas of the EC, however, allowing Denmark and the United Kingdom to opt out of the third stage of EMU and the United Kingdom to opt out of the agreement on social policy, and introducing the concept of a *derogation* in the third stage of EMU for states that do not meet the necessary criteria for adoption of the single currency. States with a derogation are committed to joining the monetary union if and when they meet the convergence criteria, yet there is no prescribed timetable for them to do so.

2.4 Depth and scope of integration: The European trade-off

2.4.1 Intergovernmentalism versus supranationalism

Since the 1950s European integration has proceeded in two different modes: a *deep*, supranational mode and a *shallow*, intergovernmental mode. Under the supranational mode, European countries have created common institutions, formulating and monitoring the impact of Community policies, and a genuine Community law interpreted by the Court of Justice and applied also by national courts. Under the intergovernmental mode, national governments have agreed to coordinate their policies, but these are implemented by national institutions, under national law, and continue to be determined to a large extent by national policy-makers. The paradigm of decision-making under the supranational mode – though not always practised – is decision by (qualified) majority, while the paradigm of intergovernmentalism is unanimity. The *depth* of integration depends both on the way common policies are decided and on the assignment of tasks to institutions. Deeper integration is characterized by decisions based on majority rule rather than unanimity and by reliance on common institutions to implement Community law and policies.

The vision behind supranationalism is that of a politically unified Europe, eventually to be endowed with the classical political institutions that characterize a state. In particular, there should be a European executive government, as well as a European Parliament and a European judicial system. Those who favour this vision argue that Europe must unify politically to meet external challenges and to ensure that disputes between European states themselves never again provide the spark for military conflicts. In contrast, the vision behind intergovernmentalism sees integration as a particularly close form of cooperation among nation states. The nation state is still regarded, however, as the highest conceivable forum of democratic political activity. Intergovernmentalism therefore aims to preserve nation states as independent entities to the largest extent possible. From its first beginnings right up to the present day, European integration has had to try to find a compromise between these two apparently opposing visions.

Since the 1950s this compromise has been sought in a trade-off between the scope and the depth of integration. The more limited a given sphere of integration, the greater was the likelihood that supranational elements could be introduced; the more open-ended a sphere of cooperation, the more likely it was that intergovernmental structures would be preserved. Thus the deep, supranational approach has been applied exclusively to economic integration evolving within the formal framework of the European Communities. Opponents of deep integration could be persuaded to give up their resistance when they saw that the supranational structures applied only where economic interdependence among the member states was easily detected, where the benefits from integration were fairly apparent and where losses of national sovereignty could be clearly limited (Collinson, Miall and Michalski, 1993). This strategic approach to starting deep integration from small but important areas was originally conceived by Jean Monnet (see Pinder, 1995).

The successful integration projects of the 1950s illustrate the point. The ECSC and Euratom were relatively narrow in their scope and had strong supranational elements in their decision-making. The EEC, which was much broader in scope, included more intergovernmentalism in its decision-making processes. The European federalists' sweeping project of a European Political Union, however, did not get off the ground in the mid-1950s, because it would have extended the supranational approach to all spheres of European integration.[10]

European governments have also cooperated, and continue to cooperate, in broader and less well-defined areas than economic policy. Such activities have evolved in the intergovernmental mode, however, and outside the formal framework of the EC. This type of integration includes European political cooperation, cooperation with non-EC states through organizations such as NATO and WEU, and even cooperation in monetary affairs through the European Monetary System.

Relaxation of the unanimity requirement has swung back and forth during the history of the Community. Since January 1966 qualified majority voting has applied, in theory, to the core areas of Community competence, that is, the common market and the common policies. Majority voting was rarely used, however, as a result of the 1966 Luxembourg compromise[11] which practically gave each member state the power to veto Council decisions.[12]

Over time, the trade-off shifted somewhat in favour of supranationalism. During the 1970s and early 1980s it became increasingly clear that unanimous decision-making in EC matters was a serious obstacle to satisfactory performance even on the economic side of integration. The SEA of 1986 partly remedied the problem by instituting new legal bases for majority voting in several areas (internal market, economic and social cohesion, research and development and environment). In these areas the rule of unanimity is confined to certain matters of special political sensitivity (such as fiscal harmonization) and to fundamental decisions. A qualified majority is generally sufficient for adopting implementing legislation. We would interpret further increases in the use of qualified majorities as a step in the direction of supranationalism. A more accurate description might be 'supergovernmentalism', since the key players remain agents of national governments and hence are only indirectly accountable to citizens.

The struggle between supranationalism and intergovernmentalism in the EU can be interpreted as a struggle between a European political elite and national political elites.[13]

Proponents of supranationalism represent a European political elite willing to give up national political interests for the sake of the common, European good and European interests. Those opposing this vision represent national political elites who wish to hold on to their domestic bases.

Initially a minority with a strong vision of European integration, the European elite adhered to a functionalist, bootstrap theory of integration. According to the model of a *cumulative logic of integration* (for example, Tsoukalis, 1977), deep integration in one area of policy creates spillovers into other areas, with the result that the participants find it desirable to deepen integration gradually in other areas. In the process, more and more national bureaucrats and national interest groups will turn to Europe to pursue their careers and interests, so that the European elite grows in numbers and influence. Over time, supranationalism permeates all spheres of European integration, and the envisioned European Union grows all by itself.

On the basis of this view, proponents of deep integration regarded every bit of supranationalism in European affairs as progress that should never be given up. They opposed all proposals to rewrite or restructure the treaties governing European integration, fearing that they might reintroduce strong intergovernmentalism in areas where supranationalism had already been achieved.

The conflict over deep versus shallow integration can also be interpreted as a struggle between the original smaller states, Belgium, Luxembourg and the Netherlands, and the larger states, most forcefully France. The former were interested in increasing the supranational elements of European integration, expecting to gain more political influence in a supranational Community than under intergovernmentalism, because weighted majority voting gives the smaller states more influence than warranted by the size of their populations. French governments from De Gaulle onwards strongly opposed supranationalism for the same reason. The fundamental importance of the Franco-German alliance to West German foreign policy led West German governments to side with France. Thus the smaller member states tended to resist reform of the EC Treaties for fear that unbundling the existing agreements would give more emphasis to intergovernmental procedures.

Until the Maastricht Treaty, the supranational branch of European integration evolved under three basic rules. First, there is the *acquis communautaire* that defines the domain of integration that has already been achieved and to which all members of the European Community must subscribe.

Second, there can be no movement back from the *acquis*. Once states have agreed to incorporate an element of European integration into the supranational framework of the EC, this element must stay there and be accepted by all future member states. Any move to deepen European integration in a particular area must, therefore, be regarded as permanent, making policy-makers very reluctant to extend supranational procedures.

It was recognized, however, that new entrants to the EC might not be ready immediately to adopt everything included in the *acquis* and, therefore, might need time to adjust. According to the *multispeed approach*, different countries are allowed to reach the *acquis communautaire* at different speeds. There remains, however, the binding commitment to adopt all requirements eventually, and to do so in a limited period of time.

Third, where conflicts occur in the political process, the principle of the *Luxembourg compromise* is that the intergovernmental mode should prevail. Even where it had been agreed before that majority rule applies, a particular state may insist on unanimity if it considers that a particular issue raises important national interests.

The Maastricht Treaty put one of the traditional EC institutions, the Council, in charge of the two new pillars of the Union: the common foreign and security policy and cooperation in justice and home affairs. The Commission is also to be 'fully associated' with the work carried out under these pillars. By giving the Council and Commission institutional responsibility in the two intergovernmental pillars, in addition to their traditional roles in governing the more supranational EC, the Treaty apparently tried to overcome the old schism between deep and shallow integration. The institutional wrap around two spheres of European integration with very different political processes, however, complicates progress in both spheres. It makes the competing political interests and approaches less visible and it will arouse suspicion that the Commission, whose institutional interest is in supranationalism, favours solutions going in that direction. Furthermore, it makes the division of responsibilities between EU bodies and national governments more fuzzy, resulting in less transparency and greater difficulty in holding different political bodies accountable. In the end the solution found in the Maastricht Treaty may, therefore, be just as likely to become an obstacle to further moves towards deepening European integration.

2.4.2   Legal disorder

The constitution of a nation state commonly provides for a hierarchy of laws, ranging from constitutional law at the top, to ordinary laws, administrative decrees and ordinances. This hierarchy embodies two kinds of distinctions. The first concerns the relevant decision-making procedure. Changes to constitutional law usually require some particulàrly heavy procedure such as a supermajority in parliament and sometimes a popular referendum. Ordinary laws usually require only a simple majority in parliament. Decrees and ordinances are administrative acts of the executive branch of government. The higher a norm in the hierarchy, the more strongly protected it is against change.

The second distinction concerns the contents of the law. A constitution typically enshrines basic principles and values, including fundamental individual rights. It also allocates authority between different institutions and, in particular, contains rules about rule-making. Simple law contains substantive rules specifying what public administrations and private citizens can do or are supposed to do. Decrees and ordinances deal with the proper administrative execution of these substantive rules. By separating formally what is of greater importance from what is of lesser importance, such a hierarchy makes the law more transparent to the citizen. Furthermore, it provides flexibility where this is needed to adapt the law to changing circumstances and needs, while protecting the basic values, rights and rules about rule-making from being changed by the air of the day.

The legal framework of the EU lacks a similar, transparent and hierarchical order. In the legal framework of European integration, the Treaties – including the protocols attached to them – are the highest form of law. They are the Community equivalent of the written constitutional document that exists in all member states apart from the United Kingdom.[14] The Treaties contain not only general principles (such as the acknowledgement of the national identity of the member states in Article F) and rules for rule-making (such as the articles creating the European institutions under Chapter E), but also substantive rules (such as the excessive deficit procedure in Article 104c) and other matters that, in a state, would properly be regulated by administrative decree. Until 1993 Part 2 of the EC Treaty was entitled *Foundations of the Community*, but this gave no special legal significance to the Articles it contained.

The lack of hierarchical order in EU law has three important consequences. First, ordinary people find it utterly confusing. The fact that citizens have no chance to learn the basic values and principles of the EU from reading the Maastricht Treaty is an important source of popular disaffection with the Union and was widely used as an argument by opponents of EU membership in Norway and Sweden.

Second, unless the Treaty itself explicitly provides for a less elaborate procedure, changing even a small detail requires a full-fledged Treaty revision including a ratification by all member states. The result of this cumbersome procedure is inevitable: European policy-makers tend to refrain from Treaty changes even where these are clearly desirable to promote the functioning of the Union.

The third consequence is political; intergovernmentalism introduces a particularly strong *status quo* bias against changing the details of a treaty once it is enacted. Since the Treaty can only be amended via an intergovernmental conference, it is too costly to make small, beneficial changes. Once an IGC is called, its agenda is potentially open-ended. Hence there is a danger that other items will be introduced into the negotiations, broadening the scope of political conflict. Moreover, proponents of change must confront the cumulative integrationists, mentioned earlier, who are reluctant to restructure the existing integration achievements. Policy-makers are thus unwilling to propose and pursue revisions in the detailed provisions of the Treaties, even when doing so is generally regarded as beneficial for the Union. The result is that the legal framework of the European Union as cast in the Treaties is excessively rigid and lacks adaptability.

2.4.3   Constitutional rigidity

The struggle between supranationalism and intergovernmentalism and the legal disorder described above have made decision-making in the European Union excessively rigid. Within its current framework, the Union has two main instruments for flexibility. The *multispeed approach* to new members was adopted in the first round of enlargements in the 1970s. The Maastricht Treaty added the concepts of *derogations* and *opt-outs* from what otherwise is a common arrangement for the remaining members. An opt-out is basically an agreement to allow a member not to participate in a certain Community arrangement, but it leaves open the possibility of opting in at a later time.[15]

The usefulness of these instruments is limited. Since the rules governing multispeed transition phases, derogations and opt-outs are part of an international treaty, a treaty revision is still needed to change them. For the country obtaining them, opt-outs, derogations and lengthy transition phases carry the stigma of being an outsider and/or a laggard, that is, they are politically unattractive.

Furthermore, an important characteristic of the current arrangements is that all member states participate in the *design* of new forms of European cooperation, even if they do not participate in the arrangements themselves; for example, the United Kingdom's participation in the negotiations over EMU. This creates a bias against the needs and desires of those who wish to participate in the new arrangement.

In short, the current instruments for flexibility to some extent facilitate negative choices, that is, they accommodate a member state's wish to abstain from certain spheres of integration if it strongly so desires. But they do not facilitate positive choices, that is, they do not provide the possibility to create new areas of integration within the framework of the EU, in which only a limited number of countries wish to participate.

2.5 Flexibility and integration in the current EU

Our discussion has characterized the development of the European Union in two important areas: the depth of integration and the degree of constitutional flexibility. In the first, we have observed a gradual movement towards more supranationalism in some areas. In the second, we have noted the requirement of strict adherence to the *acquis* and extremely low flexibility. This is illustrated in Figure 2.1. Plotting the degree of flexibility along the vertical axis and the depth of integration along the horizontal axis, the EC was originally in the south-west of this graph. Over time, the EC moved somewhat towards supranationalism and commitment. In contrast, the other elements of the EU, European political cooperation in the areas of foreign policy and home and justice affairs have remained intergovernmental.

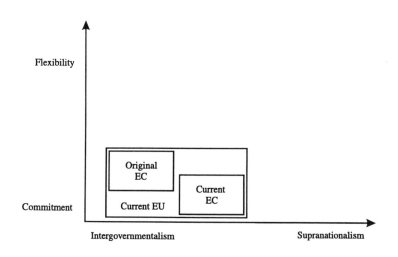

Figure 2.1 The current EU

The EU's current position in this space is unsatisfactory. It does not provide sufficient flexibility to cope with the increasing heterogeneity implied by enlargement and offers no possibility of compromise between those who wish to broaden and deepen

European integration and those who do not. In the next chapter, we discuss the options to move the Union to a better position.

Notes

1. Note, however, that Chapter 3 suggests that these transfers are not carried out in an optimal manner and that transfers are a key issue in enlargement.

2. Attempts to quantify the growth effects of European integration include Ben-David (1993), Coe and Moghadam (1993), and Italianer (1994).

3. On this point, see the discussion in Chapter 5 on how implicit internal tariffs were imposed in agriculture to compensate for currency devaluations.

4. The Court of Auditors of the EC was also raised to the status of an 'institution' by the Maastricht Treaty.

5. Under Article 148 (1) EC the general rule is majority voting unless the Treaty provides otherwise, but there are very few Treaty provisions that do not specify either unanimity or qualified majority.

6. Dismissal of the Commission requires a two-thirds majority.

7. *Costa v ENEL*, Case 6/64 [1964] ECR 585.

8. *Rewe-Zentral AG v Bundesmonopolverwaltung für Branntwein* [1979] ECR 649. The case involved the attempt to import into Germany a French liqueur with an alcohol content below 20%. German legislation required that fruit liqueurs could only be marketed if they contained a minimum alcohol content of 25%. The Court ruled that the German law could not take precedence over the Community law requirement of the free circulation of goods and, therefore, that Germany could not block the importation of Cassis de Dijon from France.

9. The Commission's right to make decisions is limited mainly to the area of competition policy.

10. De Ruyt (1987), pp. 4–5.

11. See *Bulletin of the EC*, March 1966, pp. 8–10.

12. The compromise was the solution of the first open clash between the supranational and the intergovernmental view in the episode of the *empty chair* policy, during which the French President De Gaulle had withdrawn his ministers from the European Council. See Pinder (1995).

13. For discussions of the neofunctionalist view of European integration see Pentland (1973), Webb (1983), and Keohane and Hoffman (1991).

14. For ECJ descriptions of the Treaties as a constitution see *Parti Ecologiste les Verts v European Parliament* Case 294/83 [1986] ECR 1399; First EEA case opinion 1/91 *The draft treaty on a European economic area* (No. 1) [1992] 1 CMLR 245.

15. To add to the lack of transparency and comprehensibility of these provisions, it should be noted that accession treaties ostensibly governed by the multispeed approach may contain permanent exceptions for particular member states and that the word 'derogation' is often used as a synonym for 'opt-out'. Furthermore, the legal nature of opt-outs varies. In the case of EMU, the United Kingdom and Denmark have a legal right to join the third stage if they meet the criteria. However, for the United Kingdom to join the agreement on social policy would require the relevant protocols to be amended, using the process for a Treaty amendment.

3 Combining flexibility and commitment in the EU

The challenges facing the European Union in the years to come were highlighted in Chapter 1. They are the following:

- *Enlarging* the community, making it more *heterogeneous*.

- *Widening* European cooperation to new areas as demanded by some members.

- *Deepening* European integration in the existing areas of cooperation as demanded by some members.

- *Closing the democratic deficit* of the EU by making its institutions more accountable.

The difficult task ahead is to find a constitutional framework with a proper mix of flexibility and commitment to meet these challenges. Flexibility is needed to create more room for choice in an increasingly heterogeneous Union. But more flexibility is often feared because it might undermine the substantial gains already achieved by European integration. Constitutional commitment – that is, some rigidity – is needed to protect the existing gains from cooperation and to lock in future gains where appropriate. In this chapter we argue that the appropriate mix of flexibility and commitment can be obtained only by a non-trivial institutional reform of the Union.

In section 3.1 we discuss various options for the future that have been put forward in the European discussion, including Europe *à la carte*, a European federation, multispeed integration and variable geometry with concentric or eccentric circles. We find that none of these provide the appropriate mix of flexibility and commitment. Our preferred solution, which we label *flexible* integration, is introduced in section 3.2. It combines a *common base*, where participation is compulsory for all members, with *open partnerships* that create flexibility. In section 3.3 we discuss the basic principles of flexible integration, by means of simple examples. Section 3.4 concludes with a brief summary and discussion of the institutional requirements of flexible integration, setting the stage for subsequent chapters.

3.1   Suggested paths for the future

In Chapter 2 we recalled important elements in the historical development of the EU. We showed how current EU institutions reflect a tension between two important dimensions of decision-making: supranationalism versus intergovernmentalism and flexibility versus commitment. This two-dimensional topology can be used to illustrate alternative proposals for reform of the European Union. Institutional reform can then be seen as moving to another point within the space of flexibility and depth of integration. We start by looking at two extremes of reform: *Europe à la carte* and what may be called a *United States of Europe*.

3.1.1   Europe *à la carte*

This is the most radical form of flexibility discussed for Europe today. With Europe *à la carte*, each member and all new entrants would be free to choose the areas of integration where they want to participate. There would also be no minimum degree of integration a member must accept. Members would have complete freedom to create new forms of cooperation or deepen existing ones and no barriers would keep a member from leaving a sphere of integration.

This model is attractive in that no member is constrained to accept any common policy that it dislikes. Europe *à la carte* would also facilitate and promote competition between different forms and practices of cooperation, allowing the Union to learn about their advantages and disadvantages. It would minimize the risk that forms and practices of cooperation which the members recognize are flawed – such as today's CAP – be kept alive for fear that the Union as a whole would disintegrate.

Yet Europe *à la carte* is a flawed model for a number of important reasons. As each member country would belong to different spheres, its rights and obligations in the Union would be difficult to see. The lack of transparency may trigger conflicts among the members of different spheres. More importantly, monitoring and enforcing free trade and mobility among the European countries would be very difficult. Tacit and unnoticed re-regulations of European markets could therefore destroy free intra-Union trade in small slices.

Europe *à la carte* would also create a tendency to treat participation in each sphere of integration in isolation. It would discourage, if not inhibit, beneficial deals among governments across policy areas. For example, a government might be persuaded to allow free trade in an industry exposing its domestic, uncompetitive producers to international competition, if other governments agree to free trade in financial services, where the first country is competitive. With the unstructured choice of the scope of participation and free exit from cooperative arrangements that would come with Europe *à la carte*, constructing links between different spheres would be extremely difficult. As a result, countries would be likely to agree on only a low level of integration, including a limited degree of free intra-Union trade.

Finally, Europe *à la carte* would leave efforts for free intra-Union trade and mobility with minimal protection against special interests that wish to erect barriers to trade. Currently, withdrawal from one sphere of integration implies the withdrawal from many others, if not from the Union entirely. This makes it relatively easy for governments to mobilize support in favour of a general rule of free trade against the special interests of a particular industry. But if withdrawal from a particular sphere of integration becomes possible with no further consequences, such support will be much harder to obtain, and governments will be more responsive to special interests.

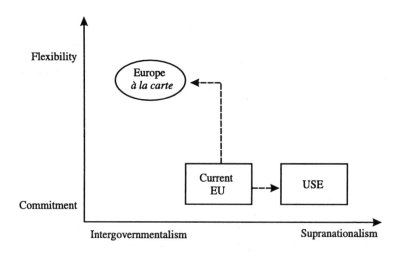

Figure 3.1 Extremes

For these reasons, Europe *à la carte* is not an attractive model for the European Union. It would destroy the Single Market over time and provide no stable solutions to the challenges Europe faces. In terms of Figure 3.1, it would move European integration to the top left corner.

3.1.2   United States of Europe

A European federal state would push the EU to the diagonally opposite corner of the figure. It would extend supranationalism to all areas of European integration and thus eliminate all constitutional variability. With the current lack of a legal hierarchy in the organization of the Union, the result would be a very rigid form of supranationalism.

A European federation would emphasize that all member countries participate on the same terms in the same areas of integration. It would have the advantage of bringing all elements of European integration under one roof. In its design, all possible bargains across policy areas could be exhausted. The scope for finding welfare improvements for all members would, in principle, be larger. Once a solution has been found, a European federation would have the advantage of protecting the gains from cooperation.

The fatal flaw of this solution is that it fails to accommodate the growing heterogeneity of the member countries' aspirations and abilities with regard to European integration; that is, to meet the challenges we have identified. A move in that direction would risk breaking up the Union, as some members would be unwilling to surrender more national sovereignty to a Europe of 15 or more member states.

Neither of these two extreme scenarios is, therefore, likely to materialize. What room is there for compromise? If compromise operates under the constraint that no major institutional reform takes place – that is, the present policy-making institutions and their mechanisms for decision-making are kept intact and the EC continues to lack a formal legal hierarchy – the compromise might involve an attempt to move in the direction of the diagonal in Figure 3.1. The deep division between the proponents of supranationalism and their opponents and the difficulty of obtaining more flexibility within the current institutional set-up, however, make it likely that this would leave all parties unsatisfied.

3.1.3   Multispeed integration

We noted in Chapter 2 that European integration has allowed countries to adopt different speeds of adjustment to the *acquis communautaire* in the past. This multispeed approach is an established procedure and some observers have concluded that it is sufficient to cope with the challenges for the future. This would have the advantage of avoiding major reform of the Union's institutions.

The usefulness of the multispeed approach as an instrument for flexibility is, however, limited. Since the rules concerning transition phases are part of the basic international treaty, treaty revisions are still needed to change them. This makes flexible choices hard to obtain. The multispeed approach clearly preserves the basic idea that there is a common level of integration and that exemptions from it are temporary and exceptional. It does not allow some countries to opt for a deeper level of integration and others to stay away from it.

Lengthy transition phases are also politically unattractive. A country that takes a long time to achieve the common level of integration would carry the stigma of being a laggard and being less developed and mature than its partner countries. Since this is an unattractive position to be in, policy-makers will strive to shorten the adjustment period. Thus the multispeed approach has an inherent tendency to provide only limited flexibility.

3.1.4 Variable geometry

A number of recent proposals for reform of the EU have tabled the concept of variable geometry as a solution. First mentioned by President Francois Mitterrand in a message to the French people on 31 December 1990, the idea has been developed by Karl Lamers, a Christian-Democratic member of the German Parliament, and by the former Prime Minister, Edouard Balladur, in a response to that paper (CDU, 1994; and Balladur, 1994). At the heart of variable geometry lies the distinction between a *core* group and a *periphery* of countries. The core includes the countries that have achieved the most in European integration, that is, those willing and able to move the furthest towards deep integration in a broad range of common policies. The periphery includes those countries unwilling or – for the time being – unable to follow the core countries and whose membership in the EU is, therefore, more restricted. The peripheral countries would participate in fewer areas of integration and do so in a more intergovernmental mode than the core countries. By its focus on countries, variable geometry takes a *geographical* approach to flexibility.

How do the proposals by Lamers and Balladur differ? The *concentric-circles* approach, proposed by Lamers, takes as a starting point a core composed of those countries that have reached the highest sphere of integration. The historical path followed by these countries defines a *fixed* sequence of steps that a country must take in order to reach the core. For example, a country that starts at the outskirts of the periphery may first have to adopt a common social policy, then monetary union, and finally a joint defence arrangement to reach the core. The result of this would clearly be a quite rigid structure. As a consequence, the decision to open a new sphere of integration would impose a very strong externality on every member of the EU, because it would affect not only a particular field of policy, but also the entire process of future integration.

The *eccentric circles*, proposed by Balladur, do not have the same rigidity. As we understand it, the proposal still focuses on the idea of a core versus a periphery of countries. It permits overlapping or non-overlapping clubs of countries, however, even though it only allows for one circle, or one cooperative arrangement, for each policy area.

Some elements of variable geometry have already found their way into the Maastricht Treaty, specifically the derogations the United Kingdom and Denmark obtained from EMU and the derogation the United Kingdom obtained from the Social Protocol. In this sense the EU has already accepted the idea.

Variable geometry has clear advantages over the *status quo* in that it allows countries to choose different degrees of membership and yet preserves the gains from integration already achieved in the Union. Thus, in contrast to the *multispeed* approach, the endpoint need not be the same for every country. In contrast to *Europe à la carte*, variable geometry stresses the notion that there is a minimum degree of communality that all members of the Union must accept. Thus economic integration in the sense of the Single Market would not be endangered by variable geometry. In contrast to the *United States of Europe*, however, variable geometry stresses the notion that not every country participates in the deepest mode of integration, leaving the possibility for some to go ahead. Furthermore, variable geometry can account for heterogeneity among the member countries. For example, countries with traditionally high propensities to inflate and weak public finances would not have to undergo drastic and painful changes to prepare for monetary union.

A flaw with this approach, most evident in the *concentric-circles* version, is to equate flexibility with different degrees of membership of individual countries. The core countries will be regarded as the elite, those who have achieved the greatest maturity and highest form of political cooperation. By implication, the countries in the periphery are laggards and immature. Thus the distinction between core and periphery implies a value judgement on the EU members that, in the end, can only be divisive. After all, who would like to be a second-class citizen? As all members will wish to be first-class citizens, the intention to introduce flexibility would fail. While variable geometry is a step in the right direction, it would be insufficient.

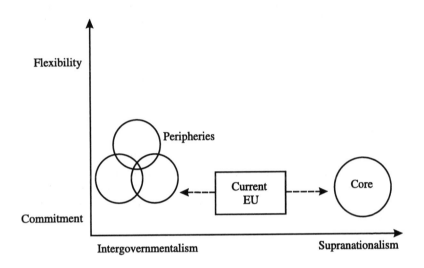

Figure 3.2 Variable Geometry

Figure 3.2 illustrates the case of variable geometry. It separates the Union into a core group moving towards deeper integration and peripheral groups moving towards more shallow integration. The focus on the quality of membership rather than flexible choice will raise the resistance of those that do not want to be second-class members. As a result, the movement could mainly be along the horizontal axis without gaining much flexibility for either group.

3.2   Flexible integration

A more promising approach is to focus variability on *areas of integration* (that is on policies) rather than *countries*. For clarity, we label this alternative approach *flexible integration*. Key to the concept of flexible integration is the distinction between a *common base* and a set of *open partnerships*. The common base contains all those policy areas over which integration is deemed indispensable for all members: it is the minimum requirement for participation in the EU and, at the same time, the largest common denominator of the Union. The open partnerships, in contrast, are voluntary arrangements for cooperation in the other policy areas. Not every country must participate in every open partnership, and members can, under some rules, set up new open partnerships or close existing ones. A key feature of this arrangement is that partnerships should not allow a subset of member states to discriminate against another one.

3.2.1 The main idea

It is important to note that our concept of flexibility is *functional*, dealing with different fields of cooperation, rather than *geographical*. All countries in the EU are members of the common base; membership in the open partnerships is optional. Thus flexible integration allows different intensities of membership in the European Union, but, in contrast to variable geometry, the focus is on policies, not on countries.

The main reason to have a base common to all members is that, as our discussion of Europe *à la carte* has shown, European integration would otherwise fall apart. Furthermore, the common base should include those areas of policy where broad package deals should be encouraged to promote the common good of all members. For example, free trade and mobility are easy and clear principles, but it is hard to agree on individual exceptions. It is thus easier to offer free trade and mobility as a take-it-or-leave-it deal to potential entrants, that is, to put these issues into the common base.

The open partnerships introduce the flexibility needed to adapt the future Union to the heterogeneity of its members. They create opportunities for experimenting with new forms of cooperation. If successful, the Union may decide that an existing partnership should become part of the base. The regulations of the base, therefore, will have to contain provisions for expanding it into new areas.

Furthermore, the common base would embody the largest communality of the Union. A well-defined common base can be organized in a supranationalist fashion. The open partnerships, in contrast, and their relationships to the common base would be governed by intergovernmental agreements among the member states. This does not preclude the possibility of the participants in a particular open partnership choosing a *deep* mode of organization for their arrangement, for example by delegating decision-making powers to a common institution as in the case of the common central bank in a currency union.

Thus flexible integration allows the Union to move in two directions simultaneously. By moving the base and the partnerships into different modes of integration and introducing a proper hierarchy of laws, the Union can overcome its current stalemate. It can appease the legitimate concerns of those who opt for the *status quo* for fear that new treaties might compromise essential elements of the European Union. It also achieves enough flexibility for countries to choose between different spheres of integration and to create new ones with other countries that have similar preferences for wider integration.

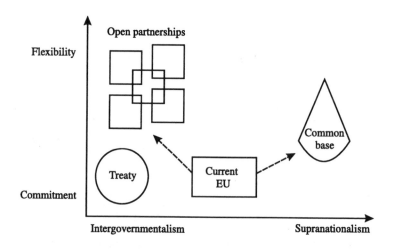

Figure 3.3 Flexible integration

Figure 3.3 illustrates the essence of flexible integration. It would move the base along the horizontal axis towards more supranationality, while the policy spheres governed by partnerships are moved towards less deep integration. Because the constitutional law of the Union is enshrined in the Treaty that locks in the basic values and rules, both the common base and the open partnerships can move towards more flexibility.

3.2.2   Organizing the open partnerships

Cooperation in a new policy area which is not in the common base could take one of two forms. The first would allow only one partnership in the new policy area. An example of this approach would be a more flexible version of the current plans for monetary union, with the current links with other policy areas spelled out in the Maastricht Treaty and the ambiguity over countries' final choice about whether to join or not being removed.

The other form would allow for multiple – overlapping or non-overlapping – partnerships in the same area. An example may be three environmental open partnerships to protect the water quality of the Mediterranean, the Baltic Sea and the North Sea, respectively. Given its location and ambitions, a country may prefer to join none, one or more than one of these partnerships.

Handling the externalities of a new partnership implies two principles. First, in order to prevent discrimination, all EU members must have some say in the design of the partnership, including its institutions. The design would thus reflect the preferences of both the immediate participants and the other members. Negotiations over EMU proceeded under this principle. The more influence is given to the non-participants, moving from simple consultation to voting rights, the more this design is likely to be driven away from the preferences of the participating countries. The second principle, giving a safeguard to non-participating members, is to agree upon the entry rules to a new partnership at the time of its formation. If the agreement of all members is required, entry requirements are likely to be at best instruments to delay the entry of countries that want to join a partnership in which they are undesired partners. This would reduce possible divisiveness created by the new partnership. The Maastricht convergence criteria are an example of such entry rules. They created less opposition than the plans for a hard core arrangement (the Lamers proposal), which aroused fears that the hard core group of countries starting with EMU would be able to change entry rules at their discretion in order permanently to exclude some countries. In Chapter 6 we discuss current and future proposals for monetary union in the light of the two principles set out in this paragraph. They create some rigidity in the formation of open partnerships.

In any case, new open partnerships require a common decision by all union members that their *formation* does not interfere with the proper working of the base and does not hurt other, existing partnerships. Within the current institutional setting, such a decision could be made by the European Council on the recommendation of the European Commission. Alternative institutions performing this monitoring role are entirely feasible. The monitoring agency would prevent countries from forming partnerships that, for instance, would reintroduce barriers to trade and mobility. Such monitoring to prevent large negative externalities between the common base and the open partnerships, or across different partnerships, would not only be needed in the formation stage but also remain necessary in the operation of the Union.

It could be argued that the difference between variable geometry with eccentric circles and flexible integration is only a matter of semantics. The core of countries under the model of eccentric circles can be a group of countries which, under flexible integration, would choose to belong to all existing partnerships. It is not unlikely that such an outcome would occur. The difference between the two concepts is, however, related not only to the stigma from which countries outside the core will suffer under variable geometry, but also to the principles for setting up open partnerships. From that point of view, variable geometry suffers from excessive rigidity, since flexibility will be implemented only through negative choices by a system of derogations and opt-outs. EMU is again a case in point. As we discuss further in Chapter 6, the EMU agreement might have been very different, in both the entry requirements and the design of the ECB, if the principle of open partnerships had been explicitly recognized at the time of the agreement. In addition, with variable geometry the EU risks evolving into a network of bilateral and multilateral agreements among states, with no clear role for the European Union institutions (Whiteley, 1994). By focusing these institutions clearly on the common base and, as we discuss below, strengthening their role within that domain, flexible integration assures that the institutional framework of the Union does not become an empty shell.

3.3 Principles of flexible integration

In this section we shed more light on flexible integration by a sequence of examples. They are meant to illustrate the benefits of being able to create open partnerships in specific areas of integration, as well as the possible tensions such partnerships may create and that appropriate institutional design will have to tackle. We also stress some of the possible inefficiencies generated by the current mode of integration in the European Union. It should be emphasized that this section is only illustrative. As stressed in Chapters 6 and 7, institutional rules are incomplete contracts that cannot foresee all possible contingencies, so that the principles highlighted here are not meant to be universal but are to be understood in reference to specific examples that have been relevant in the history of European integration.

Consider three countries – A, B and C – which have the option to cooperate by close integration of their policies in a particular area. In each of the examples below there are three possible alternatives: first, the *status quo* of no coalition; second, an open partnership between A and B; and third, overall integration among all three countries. Associated with each alternative is a pay-off to each of the countries. For ease of the analysis, we can think of these pay-offs as permanent increases in real income. We will assume that the current institutional set-up of the EU allows only the first and third alternatives and gives each country veto power against alternative three. In contrast, flexible integration will also allow open partnerships, that is alternative two, without the veto power of country C. It will also be interesting to contrast flexible integration with majority voting on the move from the first alternative to the third alternative.

3.3.1 Efficient overall integration

Let us begin with a simple case where overall integration is the preferred form of integration for every country. The pay-offs are given in the following table:

Alternative	Country pay-offs		
	A	B	C
Status quo	50	50	50
Overall integration	70	70	60
Open partnership	60	60	50

The open partnership option obviously does not add anything essential in this case.

We can think of this simple example as representing policy areas where the gains from overall integration are clear-cut and indisputable to all the countries. In a process of sequential integration, like the one in Europe in the past decades, we would obviously expect such gains to be exploited early on; it is not far-fetched to interpret the initial EEC as an instance of precisely this type of integration.

3.3.2 Efficient open partnerships: The generalized subsidiarity principle

In the example above, overall integration was the most efficient solution for all three countries. But sometimes that will not be the case. Consider the following example:

Alternative	Country pay-offs		
	A	B	C
Status quo	50	50	50
Overall integration	70	70	40
Open partnership	75	75	50

Here overall integration is more efficient in terms of *total* pay-off than the *status quo* of no integration, although country C is worse off (see below). But an open partnership formed by countries A and B is preferred by all three countries to overall integration, as well as to the *status quo*. Constraining integration to involve all countries is clearly undesirable: why not let groups of countries go along by themselves in an area of integration which they like and others do not, particularly if their cooperation does not impose any cost on others?

This can be thought of as a *generalized subsidiarity principle*: it may be preferable to decentralize some policies not only to individual countries in the Union but also to subgroups of countries. The efficient decision-making level need not always be either national or pan-European. For example, it is not clear why Mediterranean countries should be involved in the clean-up of the Baltic Sea and *vice versa*, even though each group of countries recognizes that cooperation with neighbours is desirable. Note that such environmental partnerships may have externalities for the functioning of the Single Market. Their organization should make sure they do not interfere with it.

3.3.3   Inefficient bundling across areas of integration

If open partnerships are prohibited, overall integration is still better for the Union as a whole than the *status quo*. In the previous example the total pay-off is 180, as opposed to 150. But since C is worse off with overall integration, it would veto such integration without some compensation from the other countries. This compensation could be a direct income transfer from the other two countries. We discuss such transfers, and the potential costs associated with them, in the next two sections.

First we focus on another form of compensation, namely a bargain involving another area of integration where C fares better. Suppose we find another field, where the natural partners are instead countries B and C, and with a pay-off constellation like:

		Pay-offs: Field 2	
Alternative	A	B	C
Status quo	45	45	50
Overall integration	35	70	70
Open partnership	50	70	70

If we add the two pay-off matrices, we get:

		Total pay-offs	
Alternative	A	B	C
Status quo	95	95	100
Overall integration	105	140	110
2 open partnerships	125	145	120

A bargain involving overall integration in both fields leaves all countries better off than in the *status quo*. Such a bargain would thus be struck if overall integration is the only option and open partnerships are excluded. The bargain is still inefficient, however, relative to the formation of two separate, overlapping partnerships, one between countries A and B in the first policy field, and one between B and C in the second. The cost of not permitting the generalized subsidiarity principle to operate is thus substantial in this example.

This illustration of the generalized principle of subsidiarity brings home a simple, yet important, point. If countries are heterogeneous enough in their views on further integration, the current institutional set-up of the Union, requiring every country to participate in every new form of integration, becomes a straightjacket that may force complicated and suboptimal bargains across policy fields. Allowing new partnerships to be created removes this straightjacket.

3.3.4 Open partnerships and the distribution of the gains from cooperation

In the two last examples, the ability to form partnerships leads to more efficient solutions for all three countries. A less obvious implication of the ability to form such partnerships is that it may influence the distribution of the gains from integration whether or not the partnerships are efficient by themselves. To illustrate this possibility consider an example with the following pay-offs:

	Country pay-offs		
Alternative	A	B	C
Status quo	50	50	50
Overall integration	70	70	40
Open partnership	60	60	35

Now overall integration leads to the highest total pay-off for the three countries together, the joint pay-off of 180 dominates the *status quo* of 150, as well as the 155 when A and B integrate. Countries A and B prefer overall integration to a partnership, however. So does country C, because its losses – relative to the *status quo* – are smaller with overall integration than under open partnership. Let us now add to this example the option for countries to pay each other direct income transfers out of their pay-offs.

What outcome should we expect in this situation? How is the outcome affected by the right of countries A and B to form a partnership? If income transfers between the three parties can be made without any waste of resources, we know the answer to the first question from the *Coase theorem* – a famous result from economic theory. Applied here, it says that the result of rational choices will always be the efficient outcome – overall integration in this example – independently of the legal rights of countries. These legal rights will affect the *distribution* of the total gains from integration, however.

Let us see why. If only overall integration is allowed, country C vetoes integration, unless it gets a transfer of at least ten units. Exactly how much each country gets depends on the details of the bargaining process. But the right for A and B to form a partnership alters the strategic situation considerably. It is better for C to be inside the coalition of three, rather than outside the coalition of two, and A and B are better off with partial integration than under the *status quo*. Therefore the open partnership becomes a credible threat that will make C swallow the bitter pill of overall integration without any side payments.

The situation where some countries dislike integration but go along with it for fear of being left out on the periphery of a large integrated area is instructive when considering some countries that joined the EU in the last decades. A similar bandwagon effect is possible in the future in the case of the Schengen agreement, the third stage of EMU or a defence union.

On the other hand, the move to full integration with compensating transfers has happened, for example, when the Single Market was accompanied by a doubling of the Structural Funds to help Southern European countries cope with freer trade. What the above example suggests is that the ability of northern countries to form open partnerships in the 1980s might not have prevented the Single Market but would have stopped the expansion of Structural Funds. This illustrates the potential challenges of flexible integration: as stressed in Chapter 4, it should be recognized that the Single Market, although efficient, may threaten 'social cohesion' and thus be politically unviable. In this respect, including transfer policies associated with the Single Market in the common base is an instrument to preserve social cohesion.

It is interesting to note that, in the above example, introducing flexible integration is equivalent to introducing majority voting in the integration decision. In such a case, the move to overall integration without transfers is supported by countries A and B, with C in the minority. As with flexible integration, majority voting matters here in terms of allowing winners not to compensate losers. As the next section shows, both procedures may facilitate integration.

3.3.5   Costly transfers

The assertion of the Coase theorem, that the legal restrictions are of no importance to the total pay-off of the contracting parties, presupposes that there are no transactions costs in reaching an agreement. In the context of European integration this is highly questionable. It is more realistic to assume that there are positive and significant costs involved with setting up transfer systems among the European countries, especially if the transfers are tied to particular uses; consider the CAP, for example. Let us assume that every unit transferred to country C in the previous example wastes half a unit and consider again the case where only overall integration is possible. An example of a scheme that will convince C to accept overall integration is the following:

	A	B	C
Transfers	–7.5	–7.5	10
Net pay-off	62.5	62.5	50

After the transfers have been paid out, all countries are at least as well off as in the *status quo*, so overall integration can be accepted, albeit at the cost of fewer overall resources.

In this situation the open-partnership option, or, equivalently, majority voting, becomes significant. The threat of A and B forming an open partnership now becomes a productive threat: the need to pay compensation to C via a wasteful transfer scheme can be eliminated. Integration can thus be achieved without wasting resources, but with a different distribution of the overall gains. Because the veto power of country C is diluted, country C makes a loss.

In fact, if transfer schemes are sufficiently inefficient, integration could even be blocked in the absence of open partnerships. In our example, if A and B have to sacrifice more than four units in total to transfer one unit to C, full integration will not happen with a unanimity rule!

In the above example, open partnerships are efficient because they reduce inefficient transfers. Some partnerships could, however, go in the other direction, as stressed in the next section.

3.3.6   Closed partnerships

Flexible integration can be divisive and inefficient in some cases, as the following example illustrates:

		Country pay-offs	
Alternative	A	B	C
Status quo	50	50	50
Overall integration	70	70	60
Open partnership	75	75	20

Here the partnership exerts a very strong negative externality on country C. We see that the efficient outcome of full integration would go through – without wasteful transfers – in the absence of the partnership option. But to avoid the partnership solution that A and B prefer, country C would have to bribe A and B with a – possibly inefficient – transfer.

This example could represent a potential defence and foreign policy union between the United Kingdom and France – A and B – that took a very hard line against Russia, a strategy which would be much more risky for countries like Germany or Finland – C – on the EU's eastern border.

The problem with the above situation arises only if the partnership is closed. To simplify, an open-partnership arrangement would allow A and B to go ahead with the partnership if C refuses to join, but would not allow A and B to exclude C if it wanted to join. While this principle works nicely in the example, complications start when operational entry rules have to be agreed upon. This topic is discussed in detail in Chapter 6 for the case of EMU.

3.3.7   Free-riding

In the previous example, the partnership was divisive because it imposed a strong negative externality on country C. But it is also possible that strong *positive* externalities could cause divisiveness in a union with flexible integration. The reason is that such externalities could give rise to 'free-riding', a well-known problem from economic theory. To illustrate this possibility, consider the following pay-offs:

		Country pay-offs	
Alternative	A	B	C
Status quo	50	50	50
Overall integration	80	80	80
Open partnership	60	60	90

This example can be thought of as cooperation in environmental policy, with gains from prohibiting toxic emissions that pollute the air or water common to the three countries. The highest total pay-off comes about when all countries impose the regulation. The regulation, however, imposes a burden on domestic industries and citizens in the form of costly investments in new non-emitting equipment. As is clear from the pay-off table, when the partnership option exists, country C may actually be better off by not participating, thereby imposing the cost of a cleaner environment on the others while enjoying the positive spillover effect. Suppose countries A and B have similar incentives to impose the costs on a partnership formed by the others. Then doing away with the option of forming open partnerships actually becomes a useful coordination mechanism to circumvent the free-rider problem and implement the efficient outcome.

Another example concerns countries tempted to stay out of stage III of EMU in order to engage in competitive devaluations. This very important issue is discussed in Chapters 4 and 6, where we stress the need to impose *rules of good conduct* to avoid free-riding behaviour that could threaten the common base.

To sum up, the different views policy-makers in the EU currently hold about the prospects of a more flexible form of European integration can be interpreted with reference to the examples in this section and the previous one. Some policy-makers expect externalities to be of little importance in the formation of open partnerships, while others expect them to be strong and omnipresent. To forgo the option of flexible integration in the face of these different expectations is, however, the most risk-averse response. Those fearing divisive outcomes could be convinced to agree, by making sure that all members have some rights to influence the formation, design and operation of new partnerships with strong externalities. This was discussed in section 3.2. We will return to this general theme again in Chapter 6.

3.3.8   Interest groups and cross-border coalitions

So far we have followed the common but doubtful practice of treating each country as a unified actor. In fact, pay-offs to integration in many fields are likely to be heterogeneous across different groups of citizens in the same country, particularly if the prospective form of integration is supranationalism rather than intergovernmentalism.

Suppose country C is composed of two groups C1 and C2 – for simplicity we ignore heterogeneity in countries A and B – and that the pay-offs in the example of section 3.3.4 can be broken down as follows:

		Country pay-offs	
Alternative	A	B	C1/C2
Status quo	50	50	25/25
Overall integration	70	70	10/30
Open partnership	60	60	10/25

We see that the first group in country C is the main loser from integration, whereas the second group actually gains, at least from overall integration.

Suppose that C1 is a small group of producers favoured by domestic regulation in the *status quo*, whereas C2 is the general public. The producer group will clearly lobby against integration at the domestic and perhaps at the Union level to protect its rents. If the government of country C is responsive to this special interest and the country has veto power, it will block integration, or it will try to compensate the interest group in some other way, for example by imposing a tax on group C2. In this case, introducing the open partnership option reduces the power of special interests over the course of integration in the Union and benefits the general public by reducing the resistance to integration as described in section 3.3.4. Another mechanism that would achieve the same effect would be a collective-choice mechanism at the central level that removed the decision from government representatives and allowed the cross-border majority to rule, which in this case would favour overall integration.

The example illustrates two general points. First, it shows that domestic conflicts over the benefits of integration may be decisive for the international outcome. The idea about a two-way interaction between domestic and international politics and policy-making has been stressed in recent research in political science as well as in economics (Putnam, 1988; Persson and Tabellini, 1995). Second, the example illustrates why it may be beneficial to have Union institutions, where individual citizens are more directly represented than through their national government representatives. Such institutions are necessary to build cross-border coalitions between majorities in different countries that run the risk of falling victim to regulatory capture. This issue is tackled in Chapter 7.

3.3.9 Uncertainty about the gains from integration

All the examples have assumed that the pay-offs to countries or to groups of citizens are known with certainty. In reality, the pay-offs are often highly uncertain, under future *status quo*, as well as under future integration. This is because of uncertainty about both the pay-offs to given policies and external factors affecting those pay-offs. Such uncertainty may make countries very hesitant to engage in further integration that involves a far-reaching surrender of autonomy. The cause of the hesitation is largely the fear that reversing the steps, if bad outcomes materialize, will be difficult and costly.

In this dimension, there is an important distinction between the current mode of EU integration and a reformed mode based on flexible integration. As discussed in section 3.1, the current presumption is that all integration, even in specific areas, is intended to be permanent and will be very hard to change. This is manifested in the principle of putting every agreement into an international treaty. In other words, the perceived *reversal costs* are very high under the present arrangements. Under flexible integration, in contrast, the reversal costs would be much smaller, because it would be possible to pursue new integration in the form of an open partnership, with a lot of flexibility with regard to entry and exit. This difference in reversal costs allows for more experimentation, where countries are able to scale down unsuccessful forms of integration in a less stigmatizing way.

We illustrate this idea in an example, which is slightly more complicated than the previous ones.[1]

	Country pay-offs		
Alternative	A	B	C
Status quo	50	50	50
Overall integration (good scenario)	70	60	60
Overall integration (bad scenario)	40	30	0
Open partnership (good scenario)	70	60	50
Open partnership (bad scenario)	60	30	50

In the pay-off table, the *good scenario* is equivalent to a good state of nature, whereas bad states have lower pay-offs. Think of the pay-offs as yearly pay-offs which continue for all future years.

Because the pay-offs with an open partnership and with overall integration are identical for A and B, these countries are equally willing to try both options, with B less willing than A since B's gains, relative to the *status quo*, are less than A's. If B has to commit to either an open partnership or overall integration forever, it may refuse both if the probability of the good state is sufficiently low; simple calculations show that this probability must be at least two-thirds for B to move away from the *status quo*. But if a move away from the *status quo* can be tried for a limited period of time, B may be willing to experiment since its potential losses are much smaller than they would be in a permanent lock-in. Thus there are definite benefits to reversible experimentation.

Another benefit from this kind of experimentation is that it may entail positive spillover effects. In this example, C has no risk at all from allowing A and B to try an open partnership but is at great risk from overall integration. While C would thus probably veto overall integration, even if it could be reversed after one year, it would be very supportive of an open partnership experiment from A and B since it could learn from their experience.

This example is obviously an oversimplification in that the perfect correlation of pay-offs makes learning complete. Further, there is no possibility of an *ex-post* disagreement about the desirability of integration. But the same kind of argument goes through as long as pay-offs are positively correlated and disagreement is not too strong.

There are two general lessons from this example: open partnerships allow for beneficial experimentation; and countries that are reluctant to experiment themselves can learn from the experiments of others.

This example can be viewed as the initial process of economic integration in Europe, described in Chapter 1, with a group of the OEEC countries (the initial six) going ahead with more ambitious integration than another group of (EFTA) countries, which were more uncertain of the prospective gains. Over time, the positive experience from the EEC experiment spilled over to the other countries, which gradually became convinced of the benefits from deeper and broader integration.

3.3.10   Conclusion

We have emphasized that flexible integration is a way to implement a generalized subsidiarity principle, where decentralized partnerships may give gains to subgroups of countries without hurting others. Even when overall integration is the efficient outcome, the right to form open partnerships affects the way the gains from integration are distributed. When transfers are costly, we have seen that open partnerships may operate as productive threats that reduce the size of wasteful transfer programmes. These threats can be productive, or outright divisive; to avoid undesirable consequences, non-participating countries should have a say about the formation and operation of open partnerships in fields of integration where the spillover effects can be strong and negative. On the other hand, divisive free-riding behaviour should be prevented through 'rules of good conduct' for non-participants. Finally, we have shown how open partnerships may allow for productive experimentation in the face of uncertainty about the gains in new areas of integration.

3.4   Institutional requirements of flexible integration

Flexible integration requires substantial institutional reform of the European Union. Opting for flexible integration raises the question, first, of which policy areas should belong to the common base and which can be left to the open partnerships. This question can be answered from a normative point of view – spelling out what *should* be in the common base – or a positive point of view – spelling out what the current members are *likely* to put in the common base. This is what we try to do in Chapter 4. Next, flexible integration requires an organization of the base. Particular attention must be paid to the question of how to enforce the rules protecting the valuable forms of cooperation included in the base. We discuss these questions in Chapter 5. Chapter 6 deals with the rules governing the formation and administration of the open partnerships, with particular attention to currency union in Europe. Finally, the definition of the authorities of the European institutions, existing and new, are discussed in Chapter 7.

Note

1. This example is a variation on the theme of Dewatripont and Roland (1993).

4   Defining the common base

This chapter identifies the policy areas that ought to belong in the common base of the EU. This is necessary to make our concept of flexible integration concrete. An almost empty common base would not be very different from the proposal of *Europe à la carte* criticized in Chapter 3. Conversely, the flexibility of open partnerships would be irrelevant if the common base were to incorporate all significant policy areas.

Our general criterion is that *the common base should contain policy areas for which the gains from cooperation are perceived to be large by all members of the EU*. Even though the criterion is probably uncontroversial, its practical implementation poses at least two difficulties. First, it is very hard to come up with an exhaustive list of competences that satisfy this general criterion. Second, a country is not a monolithic entity, and different groups of citizens may have different opinions about the gains or losses from coordination. This is most evident in the case of redistributive programmes, such as the CAP and Structural Funds.

To side-step these difficulties we take a pragmatic approach. We start from the *acquis communautaire*, taking into account the history and the politics of the EU and how the Union may change in the near future. Moreover, we take a *minimalist* approach. We do not pretend to come up with an exhaustive list of competences to be included in the common base. Rather, we specify a minimal set of areas that would have to be included for the common base not to lose much of its purpose, given the *acquis communautaire*. This minimalist view does not preclude a broader view of what the common base should be. There is no reason why the competences identified in this chapter could not be expanded in the future. On the contrary, as we argued in Chapter 3, experimentation with new forms of integration may well have this result.

In line with this pragmatic and minimalist approach, we consider only policy areas in the first pillar of the Union. Disagreement among member states over foreign and security policies, and over justice and home affairs, is still too sharp to imagine that policies in these areas, beyond the recognition of some basic principles, could be coordinated among all members of the EU. Moreover, within the first pillar, we conclude that the common base should include the policies that enable the Single Market to function efficiently and to be politically viable. Concretely, and with some approximation, the common base would consist of all Single Market policies, Structural Funds and some reformed version of the CAP, but neither the Social Protocol nor a single European currency.

In this chapter we also make a number of recommendations for improving policies in certain areas, given that they belong to the common base. In particular, we advocate further and more rapid reform of the CAP in the direction of income support for farmers, abandoning any form of price support, as already indicated in the MacSharry report (European Commission, 1991). We also suggest ways to enforce a mild form of coordination in capital taxation, with a view to including it in the common base.

4.1   Preliminaries

Ensuring free trade in goods, services, capital and labour has been at the heart of European integration from the beginning and has culminated in the Single Market initiative. The economic benefits of free trade are well known. But the Single Market is not only about economic efficiency. The mobility of labour also fosters political integration, because it increases communication and mutual understanding, and creates common interests and values. This was clear to the founders of Europe, and figures prominently in the preamble of the Treaties. Freedom of movement is also a fundamental civil right of individuals. For these reasons, the Maastricht Treaty's concept of *citizenship* of the Union, which includes guarantees of freedom of movement and residence for citizens, not just for labour as a factor of production, should be part of the common base.

Free trade means more than the elimination of tariffs. It also means the absence of non-tariff barriers of various kinds. This requires some coordination of industrial, regulatory and competition policies, to make sure that they do not impose tariff equivalents on goods produced in other European countries. This is the approach taken in the Single European Act. Finally, a natural corollary of free internal trade is a common trade policy *vis-à-vis* the rest of the world. These considerations lead us to a complete and operational definition of the Single Market, namely a customs union with no internal barriers to trade in goods and services and with no barriers to labour and capital mobility.

The Single Market, so defined, clearly belongs to the common base as we have defined it. It is the only part of European integration to have satisfied the general principles stressed above. Indeed, no other policy has received the same commitment from member states *in its own right*. We can think of some (not necessarily pleasant) future scenarios in which a common foreign and defence policy may receive the same priority, but it does not at this stage.

We thus take it as given that, at the present time, the common base should be organized around the Single Market. This chapter then asks a simple question. To preserve or enforce a well-functioning Single Market, do we need to coordinate *other* dimensions of economic policy among *all* member countries? If yes, then these other dimensions also belong to the common base. If no, then they are the domain of the open partnerships. The common base thus consists of the minimum set of policy dimensions needed to ensure the preservation of the Single Market over time and in a large set of (possibly very heterogeneous) countries. This means that policies should belong to the common base if they are necessary either to make the Single Market function *efficiently*, or to make it *politically viable*.

The efficiency requirement stresses potential complementarities between free trade and other policy dimensions. As argued above, free trade is naturally complemented by the centralization of trade policy. To some extent, it is also complemented by coordination of regulatory, competition and industrial policies. These policies will be at the heart of the next chapter. Complementarities also exist in many other policy dimensions, but if they are weaker or more controversial the argument for including them in the common base is less compelling.

Political viability may require compensating the losers from free trade. There is an uncontroversial presumption that free trade is efficient for the EU as a whole. Nevertheless, some participants in the Union can be made worse off by a stricter enforcement of internal free trade, by more free trade with the rest of the world, or by further enlargement. The losers could occasionally be entire countries, but are more likely to be regions, economic sectors, or groups of individuals. To prevent the losers from vetoing an efficient change of the *status quo*, it could be necessary to compensate them for their losses. An example is agriculture. To convince the agricultural lobby to abandon the current Common Agricultural Policy of price support for more efficient trade at world market prices, it may be necessary to replace it with an income support programme for farmers. It is important, however, to implement these compensating transfers efficiently and to avoid creating politically powerful lobbies that subsequently become rent-extraction machines.

Five policy areas *currently* constitute the backbone of the European Union:

- The *Single Market* in goods, services, labour and capital. This programme is accompanied by the centralization of trade policy and of some dimensions of competition and industrial policies, as well as by indirect tax harmonization.

- The *Common Agricultural Policy (CAP)*.

- The *Structural and Cohesion Funds*.

- *Social Policy*, especially the Social Charter, and the Maastricht Protocol and Agreement on Social Policy.

- *Economic and Monetary Union (EMU)*, including the plan for a single currency in the third stage.

These areas do not all share the same degree of commonality, given the UK and Danish opt-outs from the third stage of EMU and the UK opt-out from the Agreement on Social Policy.

We have already argued that the Single Market belongs to the common base and implied that the common base also includes trade policy with the rest of the world, as well as the elements of competition, regulatory and industrial policies already under the competences of the EU. The next chapter discusses in more detail the organization and enforcement of the Single Market broadly defined (that is, inclusive of these other economic policies).

We now ask whether the remaining policy areas listed above and some others should belong to the common base.

4.2   The Common Agricultural Policy and the Structural Funds

The CAP and the Structural and Cohesion Funds have four features in common. First, they both emerged as compensation schemes in the march towards internal free trade in the common market. On the one hand, they were a means to compensate the countries or groups most likely to be harmed by free trade. On the other hand, they provided an opportunity to distribute rents to politically powerful interests. The basic structure of the CAP was agreed in 1961 and the system was progressively established during the 1960s. Structural Funds came into existence when Southern European countries joined the Community, and doubled in size when the Single Market programme was instituted in 1986. The Cohesion Fund created by the Maastricht Treaty serves a similar purpose, but it is explicitly focused on poorer member states rather than regions.

A second common feature is their significance in terms of the EU budget: 50% for the CAP (mostly benefiting Northern farmers), 25% for Structural Funds (benefiting poor, and thus mostly Southern regions of the Union). Third, they both represent a challenge for enlargement towards the East in that the EU budget would double, as a percentage of EU GDP, if these programmes were kept unchanged.[1] Finally, the design and administration of CAP and Structural Fund policies have been widely criticized for poor financial management, lack of clear objectives and a Byzantine complexity that creates many opportunities for fraud, waste and inefficiency.

The nature of these two programmes is very different, though. The CAP consists of a customs union with a common external tariff, plus a price support scheme for agricultural products. There are a number of Structural Funds, with several overlapping objectives, but the main element consists of transfers for infrastructure investments in poorer European regions.[2] Let us evaluate the *organization* of these programmes as well as the arguments for whether or not they belong in the common base.

4.2.1   The Common Agricultural Policy

When it comes to the contents of the CAP, there is near unanimity among economists for moving away from price support for farm products towards *income* support for farmers. This is because trading at world market prices is more efficient. Artificially high prices induce overproduction and reduce consumption. Overproduction in turn wastes resources and damages the environment, for example through the unnecessary production and use of fertilizers and pesticides. Whatever the institutional arrangement, the CAP ought eventually to be transformed into an income support programme for farmers. Inspired by the MacSharry report, it has already started to move in that direction.

The next question is whether income support ought to take place at the national level or through the EU. There are several strong arguments in favour of national transfers. The first follows from the subsidiarity principle. Once the CAP is completely transformed into an income support programme, there is no clear externality involved, and hence it can be decentralized. Second, if the CAP is managed by the EU according to a common principle for all countries, enlargement to the East would put enormous pressure on the EU budget. Baldwin (1994) estimates that including the Visegrad countries in the CAP would more than double its expenditure, from ECU 35 billion to ECU 72.6 billion. The CAP budget itself represents more than half of the EU budget. Naturally this problem arises irrespective of whether the CAP is applied by means of income or price support. East European farmers are much poorer than EU farmers and the prices of their products are much lower than farm prices in the EU. Third, decentralization would encourage the government of each state to take effective measures against fraud, waste and inefficiency. At present, national governments face little incentive to do this. Any reduction in total EU expenditure that results from its efforts reduces all 15 national contributions to the EU budget. A typical member state thus receives only one-fifteenth of the gain from any effort it makes to curb waste. If the costs of farm support were borne directly by the state's own budget, the state would internalize the full fiscal advantage of better financial management.

The final argument in favour of decentralization is that it would make the redistribution to farmers much more transparent. At present, the CAP redistributes in favour of farmers; on top of that, because of the mechanism of compensatory amounts, some countries are net recipients while others are net payers. Hence sectoral and geographical redistributions are intertwined. Moreover, it is difficult for national taxpayers to see how their money is spent and why. Greater transparency would make it obvious that only a few benefit from a programme that imposes great distortions on everybody. This is likely to create political pressures in favour of scaling down the size of the programme and increase overall efficiency.

Precisely for this reason, however, excluding the CAP from the common base is certain to be strongly opposed by farmers. The efficient solution – transform the CAP into an income support programme and decentralize it completely to national governments – is unlikely to be politically viable. Two alternative scenarios seem more realistic.

In the first, the CAP would remain in the common base. The budget pressure from enlargement could be exploited to downsize the programme. With CAP support available to every new member, the EU would probably be forced to downsize support to farmers to a level compatible with the entry of East European countries on equal terms. National governments could, of course, develop their own income support for farmers to complement the reduced scale of support through the CAP. The risk in this scenario, however, is that the powerful agricultural lobby would persuade the EU governments to postpone, or even abandon, enlargement.

The second scenario would limit the CAP to the current EU member states. This would facilitate further enlargement, but presents two risks. First, there would be less pressure to abandon the current, inefficient price support mechanism in favour of income support. Second, given the importance of the CAP for the EU budget, East European countries would have to be refused voting rights on the CAP and related matters. In practice enlargement to Eastern Europe would thus take the form of a looser association with a group of second-class countries, which would probably be unacceptable to them. In any case, it would weaken the irreversibility of their transition to free market democracies, and thus run counter to one of the main purposes of enlargement.

While both scenarios are problematic, we feel that the political need for enlargement in an equitable way ought to receive priority. Hence the first scenario, with the CAP in the common base, is preferable. This may require living with an excessively large CAP at least temporarily. Irrespective of enlargement and of whether or not the CAP is included in the common base, its transformation into an income support mechanism should continue with urgency.

4.2.2   The Structural and Cohesion Funds

Structural Funds primarily subsidize infrastructure investment, whereas the Cohesion Fund subsidizes environmental and transport infrastructure projects. Both programmes are meant to help poorer areas of the EU reap the benefits of free trade instead of being further impoverished by it. The argument is familiar to economists from the recent theory of endogenous growth (see Lucas, 1988). This theory draws attention to the possibility that the poorer regions of the EU could continue to grow at slower rates than richer regions. Specifically, free trade could lead to growth divergence if countries specialize in sectors with different dynamic externalities: 'agriculture', for example, with no positive growth externalities, as opposed to 'high tech', which facilitates further innovation or acquisition of human capital. Infrastructure subsidies are a relatively efficient, non-distorting way to help the more undeveloped regions, much preferable to specific sectoral subsidies. A counter-argument, as in the case of the CAP, is the prospective fraudulent or inefficient management of funds. There is also a real danger that national or regional authorities may misuse the subsidies by replacing efficiency with political criteria, leading to rent-seeking activities and inefficient allocation of resources. According to conventional wisdom, the Structural Funds are useful in some countries but are clearly abused in others.

If Structural Funds are used inefficiently inside countries, they nevertheless serve a second important purpose, namely to facilitate side payments across countries so as to redistribute the gains from cooperation and to preserve its political viability. Compensating the losers from free trade is one such instance. But as discussed in Chapter 3, there are many other policy areas where the gains from cooperation are distributed asymmetrically across countries, and side payments may enable countries to reach Pareto-improving agreements to the benefit of all countries. Mainly for this reason we conclude that the Structural and Cohesion Funds ought to remain in the common base and be managed by the EU institutions.

A key issue is whether these funds should continue to be directed towards specific purposes or projects and, in the case of Structural Funds, to specific regions within states. If one of the main purposes of the Structural and Cohesion Funds is to facilitate side payments across countries, why not transform them into a system of intergovernmental transfers without any conditionality attached in terms of spending? Such a system would have three advantages. First, it would be more transparent. Second, it would avoid the problems of waste and fraud associated with national administration of subsidy programmes. Third, it would avoid a moral hazard problem now created by the Structural Funds: a state whose per capita GDP is above the qualifying threshold but which includes regions whose per capita GDP falls short of it risks losing help from the Funds if it embarks on its own egalitarian transfer or investment policies. Direct and uncontingent intergovernmental transfers, by contrast, do not distort the incentives of member states.

The problem with straightforward intergovernmental transfers is that they can become too divisive. Since they only redistribute between states, they induce political coalitions along national borders and are difficult to change without creating divisions between countries. This could strongly reduce the cohesion inside

Europe. For this reason, it is important that the transfers be set according to some 'objective' criteria, which are not easy to manipulate and which do not distort the incentives of local policy-makers.

4.2.3 Community transfers and future enlargement

As in the case of the CAP, keeping the Structural and Cohesion Funds in the common base would create a problem for enlargement. Given their low per capita GDP, East European countries would receive very large transfers from the EU if they could access these programmes on equal terms with the current member states. The resulting pressure on the EU budget is likely to improve efficiency in the allocation of these funds. But would such pressure be economically and politically bearable?

There is no doubt that the transfers necessary for enlargement would be economically feasible. Extending the CAP and the Structural Funds to the countries of Eastern Europe on equal terms would almost double the EU budget (Baldwin, 1994). But such an increase would amount to only about 1% of the aggregate GDP of the EU. Thus enlargement to Eastern Europe is a manageable problem for EU resources. The real question is whether the sacrifice is politically viable. The danger is perhaps not so much that the taxpayers would not be willing to go along; it is rather that enlargement would be postponed, because the current beneficiaries of these programmes (located mainly in the countries of Southern Europe) would be afraid that their size would be scaled down.

In the case of Structural Funds, however, this risk seems smaller than for the CAP. One reason is that the resource cost is smaller. Another is that the agricultural lobby is better organized than the many dispersed beneficiaries of Structural Funds. A third reason is that the current situation is in some ways similar to when the Structural Funds were initiated. When Spain, Portugal and Greece joined the Community the creation of the Structural Funds facilitated their participation in free trade. The benefits to the existing members of the EC were not just economic, but also political. The transition to free trade in Europe was seen as a means of strengthening new democracies in regions with recent and prolonged experiences of dictatorship. Similar political benefits are clearly present with respect to Eastern Europe today. The countries of Southern Europe cannot be deaf to this argument.

Summarizing, the difficulties of enlargement to Eastern Europe do not seem insurmountable enough to overturn our conclusion that the Structural Funds ought to be included in the common base.

4.3 Tax coordination

Does the Single Market require harmonization of taxes throughout the EU? This question arises because indirect taxes and subsidies can replicate tariffs and distort international trade. Moreover, apart from tariff-equivalent forms of taxation, the mobility of tax bases in the forms of goods, services and factors of production raises prospects of tax competition. If governments choose to reduce tax rates in order to attract tax bases away from neighbouring countries, other countries will reduce their tax rates in response, leading to further reductions, further responses and eventually to much lower taxation.

The welfare effect of such competition, however, is ambiguous. If political distortions induce excessive government spending and taxation, then tax competition can be welfare improving. Even though governments might prefer to cooperate to avoid such competition, citizens and taxpayers could be better off without any cooperation.

Notwithstanding the last point, very strong fiscal competition could endanger the political viability of free trade, possibly putting the whole process of European integration in doubt. In extreme circumstances the political majority in a country might prefer to leave the EU and bear the inefficiencies of protectionism and capital controls in order to avoid the consequences of fiscal competition (see Bolton and Roland, 1995). For tax competition to be a real threat, however, tax bases have to be very mobile. This leads naturally to a distinction between capital income taxes, labour income taxes and indirect taxes.

4.3.1 Indirect taxation

Throughout the history of the EC, an argument for harmonizing indirect taxes has been to allow the undistorted mobility of goods and services. This has led to some harmonization of tax rates on value added. Countries can now set only two rates, with a European-wide floor in each case. But in several countries VAT rates are strictly above the floors. This suggests that tax competition is not too severe. An important reason is that the consumers who would carry out the 'arbitrage' care about *net prices*, not about tax rates *per se*. Since net prices are also determined by the non-tradable components of traded goods and these could offset tax rate differences, and since there are transactions costs in doing the arbitrage, differences in tax rates can survive. The current agreement thus seems to be a satisfactory way to handle indirect tax coordination in the common base.

4.3.2 Capital income taxation

In recent years capital income tax rates in the EU have come down significantly, probably as a result of the higher mobility of financial capital. This phenomenon has been reinforced by the exemption from capital income taxation that some member states grant to non-residents. *Equity and distributional* considerations argue in favour of equal taxes on capital and labour income. From the point of view of *economic efficiency*, however, this is a controversial issue. On the one hand, a capital tax rate of zero could be inefficient, especially at a time of pervasive unemployment. Taxing labour but not capital widens the wedge between labour costs and net wages, increasing unemployment and creating distortions in the labour market. On the other hand, given the high long-run elasticity of savings and the positive externalities of capital accumulation on economic growth, capital income taxes are likely to be more distorting than labour income taxes.

Moreover, credibility problems in capital taxation could lead a government to overtax physical capital relative to labour. This is the well-known 'capital levy' problem: existing capital is the result of past savings decisions and, hence, an unanticipated capital income tax is non-distorting. A welfare-maximizing government is, therefore, always tempted to raise tax rates unexpectedly on capital and wealth, thus raising the equilibrium level of taxation. The anticipation of this reduces savings and, consequently, welfare.

Hence some tax competition may offset another distortion and improve efficiency.

Whatever the theory says, the current situation is considered unsatisfactory by most member states. Since capital taxation is a very sensitive issue, there is a serious risk of backlash against the Single Market, with some countries reinstating explicit or hidden forms of capital controls. One solution would be to tax capital income on the basis of the residence principle. This would enable each country to tax the income earned by its residents at the preferred tax rate. At the same time, tax rates could differ across localities, because tax competition would be less important. To enforce this principle, however, governments would have to *centralize information* as in the United States. That is, all financial institutions throughout the EU would have to send each national government information about the capital income earned by their respective residents. In other words, the common base would demand (at least in the long run) a fully coordinated exchange of information.

This solution would impose information-gathering costs. Most importantly, it would impose costs on Luxembourg, currently the country with the least capital taxation, since some capital would flow from Luxembourg to Switzerland or the Cayman Islands. Luxembourg could be compensated for this loss. But it should be noted that the effectiveness of coordination is the lower, the higher the prospects are for capital flight outside the EU. This pleads for negotiated agreements with neighbouring 'fiscal paradises' that have a strong interest in keeping good relations with the EU.

European countries that favour bank secrecy may well oppose the residence principle solution. In that case, an alternative policy would be to set floors for withholding tax rates on capital income across the EU, as in the case of VAT. As before, Luxembourg and possibly other countries would have to be compensated, and the effectiveness of this policy will depend on how much capital leaves the EU. But the compensation required by Luxembourg could be smaller than in the previous case, since bank secrecy would be preserved.

Whether one or the other solution is pursued, the high degree of financial capital mobility argues for putting capital income tax coordination in the common base.

4.3.3   Labour income taxation

Labour is very significantly taxed in the EU, not only through personal income taxes, but also through social security contributions. The Single Market could introduce a downward trend in labour income taxes as a result of tax competition.

There are three kinds of mobility to consider: first, individuals who change their legal residence, but not their working location (for example, they live in Luxembourg but work in Belgium); second, individuals who migrate fully; third, with mobile capital, firms that relocate to low tax areas to reduce their labour costs. The last two possibilities are more general, whereas the first applies only to a few border areas and could be dealt with by means of bilateral agreements between the countries concerned.

The only way to cope with the two more general problems would be to harmonize labour income taxes. But harmonization would also create distortions, since countries have different tastes for private versus public consumption and, therefore, want to raise different amounts of tax revenue. Tax harmonization is much more demanding than the centralization of information needed to enforce the residence principle in capital taxation. Moreover, for linguistic and cultural reasons labour mobility in Europe is not significant. Even the US states, with much more internal mobility, have large differences in their income tax rates.

Our conclusion is, therefore, that harmonization of labour income taxes does not belong to the common base. This conclusion could be reconsidered if significant evidence of divisive labour income tax competition were to emerge.

4.4 The Social Charter and the Protocol on Social Policy

In a Protocol annexed to the EC Treaty by the Treaty of Maastricht, the Agreement on Social Policy was accepted by all EU member states except the United Kingdom. The Agreement builds on the existing Social Charter[3] which had been agreed upon in 1989, again with the exception of the United Kingdom. The social protection offered by the Social Charter is quite limited compared with what is offered by national regulation in Europe. In some dimensions it is low also compared with federal regulation in the United States, where there is a federal minimum wage and a federal welfare policy. Consequently, the whole debate on labour market rigidity and on the sustainability of welfare states in Europe has focused exclusively on the *national* systems. In Europe today the Social Charter is really a set of minimum standards that are exceeded by all countries. There is, however, a concern that the Social Charter could evolve into a more binding set of centralized regulations, because the Agreement on Social Policy gives the Council power to legislate on the matters which it covers, in particular labour market regulation.

What is the argument for coordinating labour market regulation among all EU countries? As with tax competition, the fear is that free trade and mobility of capital may induce lower labour standards everywhere. The purpose of the Social Charter is, therefore, to centralize minimum standards, so as to preserve what has been achieved in the EU up to now.

It is not clear that this is a strong case, however. Drawing on our previous discussion of tax competition and the size of government, some pressure towards labour market deregulation could be beneficial, if political forces lead to excessive regulation. Given the very high unemployment rates throughout Europe, it is not necessarily desirable to preserve what has been achieved in terms of labour market regulation. The debate on this matter is still open, and the issue seems controversial.

Moreover, competition by means of lower standards of labour-market regulation – sometimes labelled 'social dumping' – seems very limited. In particular, considering labour market legislation and labour compensation in Southern Europe, it is much less of a concern than exchange rate fluctuations. The lower standards of labour-market regulation in Southern European countries do not seem to have led to trade flows as large as those induced by recent exchange rate fluctuations. Finally, strict standards in the EU could be self-defeating if East or South Asian countries treat their labour forces very differently. As with capital tax competition, the benefits of European coordination are small if outsiders do not comply.

Against these controversial benefits of centralization there are some obvious costs. Centralization of labour standards prevents differences based on national preferences or stages of development. Suppose that countries have different endowments of human and physical capital. Then, even with free capital mobility, equilibrium wages are higher in the rich countries. Forcing high minimum standards on the poor countries, as recently advocated by the Commission,[4] could impose a serious distortion: the poor countries would be forced either to leave workers unemployed, or to offer a very inefficient mix of labour compensation. This difficulty would obviously be exacerbated by enlargement towards Eastern Europe.

The conclusion is thus the same as with labour income taxation: binding minimum labour standards at the EU level do not belong to the common base at this stage. But significant evidence of social dumping in the EU could lead to a reconsideration.

4.5 Economic and Monetary Union

4.5.1 A single currency

Is Europe an optimum currency area? Few questions have received more attention in the debate on European economic integration. The conventional wisdom is that a subset of European countries may already form an optimum currency area and monetary unification among them would probably be mutually beneficial (these are Germany, Austria, the Benelux countries and possibly France – see, for instance, von Hagen and Neumann, 1994). For Europe as a whole, however, the benefits of a single currency are much more controversial. Some governments – particularly the UK government – feel that they already have a sound monetary arrangement and do not seem prepared to give up their monetary sovereignty and the freedom to pursue independent stabilization policies. Conversely, countries that may be prepared to give up their sovereignty in exchange for greater credibility to fight inflation are not seen as desirable partners: the low inflation countries (read Germany) fear that having a single common currency would then result in higher average inflation throughout Europe. In addition, enlargement would pose a particular problem for monetary union: witness the disruption caused by bringing East Germany into the German monetary system.

Our view is that the disagreement over a single currency is so strong and genuine that, at least for the time being, it should be left out of the common base. After all, this is what the opt-out clauses of the Maastricht Treaty already entail.

4.5.2 Competitive devaluations

There is, however, a fundamental difficulty. The recent monetary events in Europe indicate that nominal exchange rate stability is very difficult to achieve, short of going all the way to a single currency. But under flexible exchange rates, competitive devaluations could eventually undermine the Single Market. This is an example of the negative externalities mentioned in Chapter 3 that need to be monitored. Between September 1992 and March 1995, for example, the Italian lira depreciated by more than 60% against the Deutschmark. This huge depreciation was not accompanied by significantly higher inflation in Italy than in Germany. Average nominal wage growth, in particular, was only a few percentage points higher in Italy than in Germany. Thus, even though the depreciation was not deliberate, it boosted Italian competitiveness at the expense of Germany and the countries pegging to the Deutschmark. Spain's and Sweden's currencies have also undergone large depreciations, albeit smaller than Italy's. It is doubtful that events of this sort can continue without seriously disrupting the Single Market.

This problem is not new, even though the expansion of intra-EU trade has made it even more relevant today than it was 40 years ago. Efforts to avoid competitive devaluations have been at the core of European integration since the 1950s. The views of the political leaders that guided Europe after the second world war were influenced by the experience of the 1930s. During that decade many countries had attempted to shift the costs of the recession onto their neighbours, thus producing the collapse of the world trading system, and – in the eyes of many observers – creating the conditions for the rise of totalitarian regimes.[5] This explains why the reference to stable exchange rates is one of the first objectives written into the Treaty of Rome in 1957.

The need for stable exchange rates also resulted from the early development of the EC. Throughout the 1960s one of the main activities of the EC was the management of the common market for cereals, which was dependent on the stability of bilateral exchange rates. In the common agricultural market each commodity has a single price that is centrally set, in ECUs, by the Commission. In 1969, at the time of the first devaluation of the French franc relative to the Deutschmark, German farmers resisted a reduction in the Deutschmark price of grains, while the French government resisted an increase in the corresponding franc price in an attempt to offset the inflationary consequences of the devaluation. The outcome was a temporary suspension of the common market: a tax was introduced on French exports of grains to Germany, while German farmers received an export subsidy that compensated them for the lower price at which they could sell their products in France. The system that was set up goes under the name of 'compensatory amounts' – a soft name for tariffs. The mechanism is identical to a tariff, the only difference being its budgetary consequences: the revenue from the export tax is paid into the EU budget, which in turn pays for the export subsidy.

This way of dealing with devaluations became common practice in the EC. Since then each devaluation has been accompanied by a corresponding adjustment in taxes and subsidies on agricultural commodities. The tax introduced on the exports of the devaluing country is not permanent. As domestic prices increase, following the devaluation, the need for the tax vanishes; and so does the need for a corresponding subsidy on the country whose currency was revalued.

Compensatory amounts have recently been advocated for goods other than agricultural commodities as a way to deal with the large exchange rate changes that have occurred within the EU since

September 1992. Such requests seem to confirm the wisdom of the 'fathers' of the EC, who thought that economic integration required exchange rate stability.

We conclude that some mechanism to coordinate monetary policy between the member states of the EU has to be found. This form of monetary policy coordination, possibly weaker than constraints on nominal exchange rates, would then have to belong to the common base of the EU. The design of such a coordinating mechanism is extensively discussed in Chapter 6.

4.5.3   Competitiveness versus productivity

The previous section argued that large fluctuations in competitiveness, that is, in real exchange rates, interfere with the common market and could eventually lead to serious disruptions. But why focus only on nominal exchange rates as sources of changes in competitiveness? Should we not also worry about a country that improves its competitiveness by enhancing productivity through labour market or microeconomic policies? If so, is there not a contradiction between our conclusion that the Social Charter should stay out of the common base, and yet the common base should include some device for preventing competitive devaluations?

Let us consider a concrete example. Assume that nominal exchange rates are constant, and that the unions in a particular country accept new labour or industrial policies that cut waste and inefficiencies or lead to a better utilization of capital and labour and result in a lower unit labour cost in a specific sector. Assume also that the industry is quite competitive, so that the cut in labour costs translates into a reduction in prices. Is there a case for preventing consumers throughout the Union from benefiting from lower prices? In other words, should governments refrain from engaging in this kind of efficiency-enhancing policy or prevent firms which face a reduction in labour costs from driving down the price of their products throughout the Union?

The answer is no. The argument is similar to that used in section 4.4 to suggest that the Social Charter should not belong to the common base. We should not confuse competitiveness and productivity. The introduction of compensatory amounts in this case – a tariff on imports from the more efficient country – would prevent the cost reduction in one country from forcing other countries to match the productivity increase or cut wages. This means that there will certainly be pressure on governments to introduce such a tariff – as when cheap labour and high productivity in South-East Asia drive European firms out of a particular market – but that such pressures should be resisted.

This situation is quite different from a reduction in real wages produced by unexpected inflation, or by an unexpected devaluation. In such a case the improvement in competitiveness is not the result of a conscious agreement between firms and unions, which are caught by surprise. Thus it will not last in equilibrium. If unions can be caught by surprise, they will consider this possibility at the time of signing the contract and ask for higher nominal wages. The outcome of this 'game' between the authorities and the unions will simply be higher inflation, with no stable reduction in labour costs. Thus the authorities would be better off if they could commit themselves in advance not to use monetary policy to try to reduce real wages.

A second important difference between changes in the exchange rate and changes in labour productivity is that the former occur abruptly, whereas the latter accrue slowly over time. Thus workers in the industry of the less productive nation have more time to adjust and to relocate than in the event of an appreciation induced by sudden exchange rate changes. This difference in the required speed of adjustment has important implications for the capacity of a government to resist political pressures. Intervention through tariffs or other forms of external protection is more likely if there is little time for the domestic industry to adjust.

There is a third difference. While better competitiveness owing to higher domestic productivity increases overall production and thus improves efficiency, a devalued exchange rate simply reallocates production across countries with no net gain for Europe or the world as a whole.

The lesson to be learned from this discussion is that attempts to increase competitiveness *per se* are not undesirable. On the contrary, they may stimulate productivity and efficiency. What should be avoided are attempts to improve competitiveness through the discretionary use of monetary policy, or through policies that merely reallocate production across countries.[6]

4.6   Social insurance and regional risk-sharing

It is often argued that if and when the EU has a single currency, European countries will need to insure each other against country-specific macroeconomic shocks (see, for instance, Sala-i-Martin and Sachs, 1992; and Eichengreen, 1990). At present, these shocks can be dealt with by changing the nominal exchange rate. But once exchange rates are irrevocably fixed, how can countries deal with idiosyncratic shocks? A possible answer would be to centralize, to some extent, social and unemployment insurance. A centralized federal tax-transfer system is precisely the mechanism that provides risk-sharing between the US states.

Partial centralization of social insurance could also have beneficial political effects. It would reinforce the principle of mutual solidarity among European countries and citizens and it would establish a direct link between individual citizens and EU institutions, thereby fostering integration and inducing cross-border political coalitions.

Establishing a European social insurance system, however small, would entail a major shift away from the current mode of operation of the EU. Moreover, once created, political forces could lead to further and excessive expansion. These forces would be strengthened by the large asymmetries in average per capita incomes across Europe: a centralized social insurance system would necessarily entail a lot of regional redistribution and not just the insurance of regional or individual risks (see Persson and Tabellini, 1994).

An alternative and less radical innovation would be to share macroeconomic risks by means of intergovernmental transfers contingent on macroeconomic shocks. Redistribution and risk-sharing would still be intertwined, but the redistribution would be more transparent. Further expansion of the programme would probably also be easier to keep under control. However, identifying the macroeconomic shocks would be very difficult and yet critical to obtain welfare improvements.[7] One possibility would be to make the transfers contingent on deviations of some measurable aggregate real variable from trend. But that would be extremely arbitrary. Moreover, it would run into the moral hazard problems discussed in section 4.2.2 (see also Persson and Tabellini, forthcoming).

This issue is not on the table now, however, and it will not become relevant until the plans for a common currency become a reality.

4.7   Concluding remarks

This chapter asked which policy areas ought to be included in the common base of a reformed EU. Once a policy area is included in the common base, all member states would accept a considerable transfer of sovereignty to the EU institution that enforces policy coordination. Hence a policy area should be included in the common base only if the gains from cooperation in that area are perceived to be large by all countries in the EU. This criterion was made more operational by suggesting that the common base should include the Single Market and those other policy areas that would be needed for the Single Market to function efficiently and be politically viable.

Concretely, this identifies a common base, consisting of: the Single Market inclusive of trade policy plus those aspects of competition, regulatory and industrial policy that are already under the competences of the EU; the Structural and Cohesion Funds; harmonization of VAT; possibly a reformed version of the CAP; a mild form of coordination over capital income taxes; and a mechanism for coordinating monetary policy to avoid competitive devaluations.

The list of competences is certainly not exhaustive. There are some other policy areas currently under the joint competences of the EU and of member states, such as research and development or transportation policies, that we have not explicitly discussed, but for which a case could be made to include them in the common base. However, we have deliberately excluded from the common base two important components of the *acquis communautaire* as defined in the Maastricht Treaty. They are the Social Charter and the single currency. In our opinion, these two policy areas do not meet the requirement of presenting uncontroversial gains from policy coordination for all countries. Finally, in our view the common base would not include any policy area in the second and third pillar of the EU, with one exception. As discussed in Chapter 1 section 1.5, the common base should include an explicit acceptance of some basic principles in these areas: democratic government, human rights, mutual non-aggression and the rule of law.

Notes

1. Baldwin (1994) provides a detailed quantitative discussion of this matter.

2. The funds are: European Regional Development Fund, European Social Fund, EAGGF (Guidance Section), Financial Instruments for Fisheries Guidance. Six objectives are specified by the current regulations; see Council regulations 2052/88 OJL 185/9 1988, and 2081/93 OJL 193/5.

3. Not to be confused with the European Social Charter of the Council of Europe.

4. In the White paper on 'Preparation of the Associated Countries of Central and Eastern Europe for Integration into the Internal market of the Union' (2 May 1995), the following argument is presented: 'Another reason for legislating at the Community level has been the need to create and maintain equal conditions for economic operators. Competition could be distorted if undertakings in one part of the Community had to bear much heavier costs than in another and there would be a risk of economic activity migrating to locations where costs were lower. Such costs include those imposed on governments and economic operators by measures of environment, social and consumer protection. The implementation of high common standards of protection is among the Union's objectives and at the same time helps to ensure this "level playing field".'

5. For an account of the inter-war experience as seen from the perspective of the late 1940s, see Nurske (1949).

6. A difficult case would arise, however, if the unions in one country accepted an *ex-post* reduction in real wages produced by an unexpected devaluation. Such a situation defies rational behaviour on the part of the unions; however, it may well be that the sense of crisis that often accompanies a devaluation induces a shift in public opinion – which becomes more prepared to accept economic arguments – thus also influencing the unions. Should such a devaluation be ruled out? Some would argue that it should not: it is precisely the crisis associated with the devaluation that produced

the desirable and welfare-improving, long-lasting reduction in real wages. Others would argue that the reduction in real wages will be short-lived: as the sense of crisis vanishes, unions will demand compensation for having been 'cheated' on the commitment not to devalue. This remains an open question with no clearcut answer. We note, however, that this is precisely the situation that the EU faces today *vis-à-vis* Italy. The lira was pulled out of the ERM only weeks after the government had signed an agreement with the unions in which all wage indexation clauses were abolished and nominal wages were preset for the next two years. The agreement had been signed in a situation of urgency, in which the government repeatedly used the argument that in the absence of an agreement the lira would not survive the speculative attack to which it was subject. The agreement was signed and, nonetheless, soon after the lira was devalued. Three years on the unions have not yet asked for compensation for the loss of real wages, in part because their behaviour has kept inflation low, thus dampening the impact of the devaluation on consumption wages. We do not have an answer to this special problem. We only note that the outcome, so far, has been a reduction in Italian real wages, so that there is no clearcut case in favour of policies – such as a tariff – that would prevent European consumers from benefiting from low-wage Italian products.

7. von Hagen and Hammond (1994) show that regional real incomes could be destabilized if the shocks to which transfer payments are made contingent are not correctly identified.

5   Implementation and enforcement of the common base

Flexible integration makes it easier to implement and enforce the rules of the common base. This is one of its most important merits. Once we acknowledge that the policy dimensions of the common base are all essential for the Union, we have to be serious about ensuring that genuine integration takes place. This means that the rules necessary for the working and the survival of the common base must be observed.

At present the degree of implementation and enforcement of Community law across the EU is unsatisfactory. Among other things, lax implementation and enforcement prevent the realization of the vision underlying the Single Market programme. This is partly the result of current institutional arrangements, which limit the transfer of sovereignty from member states in many policy areas. The power to make many of the most important decisions is assigned to intergovernmental bodies, such as the Council, which are often required to act by unanimity. Narrowing down the common base to a smaller set of competences over which the gains from cooperation are large makes it possible to expect a bigger transfer of sovereignty over these competences. We discuss proposals to improve the effectiveness of European institutions in Chapter 7. In this chapter we consider how to improve implementation and enforcement of the common base, focusing entirely on the example of the Single Market. The first two sections offer a view of the facts and of the relevant procedures. Section 5.3 is devoted to the economic and political theory which supports the recommendations made in section 5.4.

5.1 Law and administration in the Community

As shown in Chapter 2, the budget of the Community and the number of Commission civil servants have both grown over time. Compared with member states, however, the Community still spends relatively little and employs relatively few people. Law is the main instrument through which its policies are pursued. Furthermore, Community law is mostly put into effect and enforced *indirectly* by the administrations of the member states (see Daintith, 1995).

The EC Treaty contains legal obligations with respect to the common market and the common policies. In order to attain its objectives, the Treaty also provides for legally binding acts to be issued mainly by the Council and Commission in the form of regulations, directives and decisions.

The fundamental difference between regulations and decisions on the one hand and directives on the other, is that only the latter require national implementation legislation. This has both advantages and disadvantages. The main advantage of directives is that they are in harmony with the principle of subsidiarity. Their main disadvantage is that implementation may differ widely across member states.

The Treaty does not distinguish between legislation, administrative rules and individual administrative acts, but the various Community acts are usually called 'legislation' or 'secondary legislation'. The Treaties, Community legislation and the jurisprudence of the European Court of Justice form the core of the Community legal order.

The rest of this section reviews the implementation and enforcement of Community law in three areas: the Single Market legislation, 'state aids' (that is state subsidies and similar measures) and mergers.

5.1.1   Implementation of
Single Market legislation

The original Treaty of Rome provided for the establishment of a common market allowing the free circulation of goods, services, labour and capital. Implementation required the adoption of appropriate legislation by the Council, based on proposals from the Commission. When the 12-year transitional period for the establishment of the common market ended on 31 December 1969, many obstacles to free circulation remained owing to insufficient enactment of Community legislation.

The Commission's 1985 White Paper *Completing the Single Market* set out a detailed legislative programme containing 270 measures intended to remove all remaining barriers to the mobility of goods, services, labour and capital. It was accompanied by a revision of the Treaty stating that: 'The Community shall adopt measures with the aim of establishing the internal market over a period expiring on December 31, 1992 ...' (Article 8a).

As of April 1995, 259 of the 270 White Paper measures had been adopted by the Council. These translate into 273 legislative dispositions, including 219 directives requiring transposition into national law. According to the Commission (Commission of the European Communities, 1995b), 92% of the measures required in order to implement the Single Market had been adopted by the 12 states that were members of the EU at the end of 1994. National transposition varies significantly between states, reaching 98% in Denmark, but only 86% in Greece. As a result, the number of directives transposed correctly in all 12 states was only 156 out of 219, or 71% of the total.

National transposition varied even more across sectors, ranging from 100% in areas such as motor vehicles, chemical products and excise duties, to 70% in fields such as information services, intellectual and industrial property, and public procurement.

The situation was particularly unsatisfactory in public procurement, where eight directives had been adopted since 1988. Derogations granted to Greece, Portugal and Spain in respect of three directives meant that 87 (8 x 12 – 3 x 3) national transpositions were required by the June 1994 deadline for the last directive. As of April 1995,

62 (71% of 87 or 65% of 96) national transpositions had been notified to the Commission, but only 45 (52% of 87 or 47% of 96) had been carried out properly. Consequently, none of the eight public procurement directives had actually been put into effect in all 12 states, and only one had been correctly transposed in all of the nine states that enjoyed no derogations.

The situation was also far from satisfactory in insurance services. Nine compulsory directives had been adopted since 1987. Since no derogations apply, 108 national transpositions were required by January 1994, the deadline for implementing the last directive. As of April 1995, 87 (80% of 108) national transpositions had been notified to the Commission and actually been incorporated into national laws. Yet only two of the nine directives on insurance services had been transposed in all 12 states. By contrast, six out of the seven banking directives whose deadline had expired were correctly transposed in the 12 states by April 1995.

The Single Market cannot be established merely by the enactment of Community legislation and its transposition into national law. There must also be effective application and enforcement of the law by member states. No systematic information is available on the enforcement of Single Market legislation, but anecdotal evidence suggests that there are problems. There is a widespread belief that effective enforcement varies a great deal between states. This undermines the credibility of the whole exercise.

5.1.2   State aids

All governments provide subsidies or other forms of aid to firms. These may distort competition within the EU, causing serious difficulties for the creation and maintenance of the Single Market. In principle, there are two ways of tackling the problem. The first would be to formulate a common industrial policy at Community level. In so far as this involved aid to firms, the aid would be granted by Community institutions from the Community budget. The second is to allow member states to continue formulating national policies and granting state aids, but to establish a system of Community supervision. The latter option was the only politically feasible one when the EEC was created.

Article 92 of the EC Treaty declares that: 'Save as otherwise provided in this Treaty, any aid granted by a Member State or through State resources in any form whatsoever which distorts or threatens to distort competition by favouring certain undertakings or the production of certain goods shall, in so far as it affects trade between Member States, be incompatible with the common market'. This general principle is qualified by exceptions *de jure* and by discretionary exceptions which cover a wide range of situations. The responsibility to control state aids and apply the discretionary exceptions lies with the Commission. Until the late 1980s the control of state aids was fairly relaxed. In 1989 the Commission published its *First Survey on State Aids in the European Community*, which revealed the magnitude of the problem. In the period from 1986 to 1988, the member states disbursed state aids equivalent to 2.2% of EC GDP, ranging from 4.1% of GDP in Luxembourg to 1% of GDP in Denmark. At the same time, aids to the manufacturing industry amounted to 3.8% of its value added, ranging from 15.7% in Greece to 1.9% in Denmark.

The Commission's lax attitude is confirmed by a recent econometric study. Neven (1994) analyses the evolution of state aids to the manufacturing sector in ten EC member states in the period from 1981 to 1990. He estimates a regression model where the intensity of state aids is related to domestic political-economy variables such as the weakness of government, its ideological orientation and the concentration of manufacturing industry. Neven finds that these variables explain most of the intertemporal and cross-country differences in state aids, suggesting that domestic politics plays the key role in determining the amount of state aids that a country disburses. By implication, the Community seems to have played, at best, a very minor role during this period.

Prompted by these and similar findings, the Commission decided that a very substantial strengthening of the system of control was required to ensure the effective completion of the Single Market. In the late 1980s it introduced more stringent procedures including systematically ordering the recovery of aids that had been paid illegally. The Commission is dependent on national administrations to ensure repayment, however; it has no power to take action against firms directly. In the 1990s the Commission's more active state-aids policy faced a rising number of politically sensitive cases, prompted by the worldwide recession and the massive restructuring caused by completion of the Single Market. Currently, the Commission and the member states are deeply split between those that favour tighter enforcement of Community rules about state aids, and those that argue for a more relaxed attitude.

5.1.3 Merger control

The 1989 Merger Regulation[1] is an interesting institutional example of implementation of a common policy. It is part of competition policy and stipulates that 'concentrations' between firms with a combined worldwide annual turnover of at least ECU 5 billion fall under the jurisdiction of the European Commission provided that less than two-thirds of the parties' European activities are conducted in a single member state. The Commission is required to block concentrations that would 'create or strengthen a dominant position'. While the regulation does not provide specific guidelines for the analysis of dominance, it is intended to benefit consumers; productive efficiency is an acceptable rationale for a merger only if it benefits consumers and does not reduce competition. Speed is a central objective of the regulation and cases of no significant concern for competition must be cleared within a month. Other cases proceed to a second stage for more detailed analysis. A decision must be made within four months.

Notice that the rule establishing jurisdiction is explicitly based on an assessment of the existence of international spillovers. It allows firms to face a single EU regulator instead of several national ones. Moreover, this regulator is best able, at least in theory, to take into account the nature of competition in the Single European Market.

The Merger Regulation has been the subject of a detailed investigation by Neven, Nuttall and Seabright (1993), who also surveyed a number of firms to assess their views on the process. There is widespread agreement that the procedure is conducted in a timely fashion. However, the positive assessment of the firms could also reflect excessively lax standards. The consensus view is that standards have certainly not been too tough. In only two cases so far has a merger been prohibited. The more celebrated case involved the aircraft makers Aérospatiale/Alenia/de Havilland. In a number of other cases the merger was accepted subject to conditions such as horizontal or vertical de-integration, divestment, or measures intended to stimulate actual or potential competition (see Neven *et al.* for details).[2] Nonetheless, the overall picture remains one of relatively lenient competition standards, despite the Commission's formal mandate to give a higher weight to consumer than to producer interests in its decisions. This apparent discrepancy between the stated goal of the regulation and the practice will be further discussed in the next section.

5.2   The existing procedures

In this section we review the existing legal procedures for taking action against states (in relation to the enforcement of Single Market legislation); Community institutions (mainly in the area of the enforcement of the rules on state aids); and private parties (mainly as regards the rules about competition and mergers).

5.2.1   Actions against member states

Who can take action and how, and what are the sanctions? The Treaty allows for actions against member states in three situations: when a state fails to transpose directives into national law; when a state fails to enforce Community law against private parties, or against public bodies of various kinds; and when a state itself acts in ways contrary to Community law.

If the Commission (Article 169) or another member state (Article 170) thinks that a member state is in breach of Community law, it may bring the matter before the Court of Justice. If the Court rules against the state, the state is required to take the necessary measures to comply with the judgement (Article 171).

Member states have been reluctant to bring proceedings under Article 170; only one case has ever proceeded to judgement under this provision (see Wyatt and Dashwood, 1993). Article 169, on the other hand, has been used frequently by the Commission. Its effectiveness, however, was hampered by the absence of any power to impose a sanction on a member state if it failed to comply with a judgement of the Court. This problem has been partly remedied by an addition to Article 171 made by the Maastricht Treaty, which allows the Court to impose a fine on a member state for failure to comply with a judgement. A number of problems remain, however. First, the process is lengthy. A fine can be imposed only after two sets of proceedings (one by the Commission, or a member state, under Article 169 or 170; then another by the Commission under Article 171 for failure to comply with the Court's judgement). Each set of proceedings involves a reasoned opinion from the Commission, with the possibility of a reply from the member state. Second, there is no provision for enforcement of the fines by withholding payments from the Community to the member state or by any other means. Third, the process is discretionary; the Commission is not obliged to take action under Article 171 if a state fails to comply with a judgement of the Court.

The Commission publishes a yearly report on infringement procedures. The reports indicate intense activity by the Commission based on Article 169. In 1994 it initiated 974 infringement procedures, sent 546 motivated opinions to member states, and brought 89 cases before the Court of Justice.[3] About 80% of the actions taken by the Commission under Article 169 resulted from complaints submitted by private parties.

Private parties can submit complaints to the Commission, with a view to its taking action under Article 169.[4] Individuals also enjoy rights under Community law to which national courts must give effect, even if there is a conflict between national law and Community law. Through Article 177, private parties also have indirect access to the Court of Justice because a national court may – and in some circumstances must – ask the Court to give a 'preliminary ruling' on matters concerning the interpretation of the Treaties and the interpretation and validity of Community legislation. The Court's decision on these matters is binding on national courts.

The Court of Justice has developed a number of principles which limit the possibility of 'selective exit' by member states from their obligations under Community law (see Weiler, 1991). Even if a state fails to transpose a directive into national law, the directive may have 'direct effect'. That is, it may create individual rights against the state which national courts must enforce despite the failure to transpose the directive. National courts must also interpret national law as far as possible to be consistent with

Community law. The 1991 ruling of the Court of Justice in the *Francovich* case[5] provides an additional possibility for private parties to seek a remedy if a member state fails to comply with its obligations under Community law. This case involved a directive to protect employees against the insolvency of their employer, which Italy had failed to transpose into national law. Employees who were owed money by their insolvent employers sued the Italian state in national courts. The Court of Justice confirmed that Community law requires national courts to give individuals a right to damages against the member state in such circumstances. Even so, a number of conditions have to be fulfilled and the full scope of the *Francovich* principle remains uncertain.

The Maastricht Treaty also recognized citizens' 'right of petition'. Citizens may submit petitions to a special committee of the European Parliament on any matter falling within the sphere of EC competences. The Treaty also provides for the European Parliament to appoint an ombudsman to investigate citizens' complaints of maladministration by Community bodies. The first ombudsman was appointed in July 1995. The effectiveness of these mechanisms, however, is limited by two main factors: they do not result in binding legal acts; and European citizens are largely unaware of their existence.[6] We return to this issue below.

Enforcing Single Market legislation. The procedure is that initially a directive must be transposed into national law. This requires three steps: first, member states must inform the Commission of the transposition; second, the Commission verifies the conformity of national implementing measures; and third, the Commission pursues infringements – for lack of transposition or non-conformity – through the formal proceedings of Article 169. At the end of April 1995, 18 infringement proceedings initiated by the Commission for non-conformity were pending before the Court of Justice, including four in the area of public procurement.

Penalties and remedies in the case of infringements depend on the national legal system and the national implementing legislation. This is a weak point of the system of indirect administration of Community law, because the effectiveness and dissuasiveness of the penalties and remedies available differ widely among member states. The result is considerable diversity in enforcement practices. This problem has been particularly acute in the area of public procurement. To tackle it, a directive was introduced to ensure a minimum level of legal protection of individual rights throughout the Community. The directive still permits wide discrepancies among states, however, with some compensating only bidding costs, while others go as far as imposing compensation for the profit that would have resulted if the contract had been awarded.[7]

Enforcing the control of state aids. The procedure for new state aids is as follows: first, member states must notify the Commission in advance of any plans to grant or alter aid; second, the Commission examines the compatibility of the proposed aid with the common market including applying the discretionary exceptions; third, if the Commission finds that a proposed aid is not compatible with the common market, the state must not put it into effect.

There are several weaknesses in this procedure. First, Commission findings on the compatibility of state aids are adopted by a majority vote of its members. Typically, commissioners vote in favour of allowing aids granted by their own member states, which produces log-rolling. Second, although it is illegal to implement an aid without giving prior notification, Community law does not allow the Commission to order repayment of an aid simply because it has not been notified; it must examine such cases – if and when they are discovered – as if the aid had been notified. Commission decisions on aid that has already been given, and which it finds to be incompatible with the common market, now always include a clause instructing member states to recover from the relevant party – in accordance with national law – the aid illegally disbursed. National courts, however, take different views about how far legal principles such as the protection of legitimate expectations prevent the recovery of such aid. In theory, there are opportunities for private enforcement by competitors against states which grant aid illegally, but knowledge of such opportunities is limited.

5.2.2   Actions against Community institutions

Actions against Community institutions should be considered when the Commission fails to enforce Community law against member states or private parties; and when Community institutions themselves act contrary to Community law. This might include, in particular, seeking illegitimately to expand the competences of the Union.

Only the Court of Justice has the authority to declare a Community act invalid. Article 173 of the Treaty provides for judicial review on the following grounds: lack of competence, infringement of an essential procedural requirement, infringement of the Treaty or of any rule of law relating to its application, or misuse of powers. The acts of a Community institution may be challenged before the Court by member states, the Council and the Commission. The European Parliament and the European Monetary Institute have a more limited jurisdiction to use Article 173. Private parties may use Article 173 only to challenge decisions addressed to them or decisions which are of direct and individual concern to them. For example, the beneficiary of a state aid may challenge a Commission decision that the aid is incompatible with the common market and, in some circumstances, competitors may challenge a decision to allow an aid to be granted.

While Article 173 provides a procedure for annulment, Article 175 can be used to pursue a Community institution for failure to act. Actions may be brought by the member states, the Council, the Commission, the European Parliament, the Court of Auditors and the European Monetary Institute. The scope for actions brought by other parties is very limited. It remains an open question whether Article 175 may be used to challenge the Commission or the Council for failing to adopt measures that would be necessary for the establishment of the Single Market in breach of the obligations imposed by Article 8a of the Treaty. For example, according to Wyatt and Dashwood (1993), failure to adopt the legislation required to permit the free circulation of goods carries greater risk of an adverse ruling under Article 175 than would a similar failure in the area of the free mobility of persons.

5.2.3   Actions against private parties

The Treaties, regulations and decisions may directly impose obligations on private parties; that is, individuals and firms. Transposition of directives into national law may also create such obligations. In areas other than competition law, the authority to enforce private parties' compliance with obligations arising from Community law generally belongs to the member states, not the

Commission. If the Commission believes that a member state is failing to ensure the proper enforcement of Community law, its only legal remedy is proceedings against that state under Article 169.

In some instances provided for by the Treaty or Community legislation, however, the Commission possesses specific enforcement authority with respect to individuals. The most important such area is competition, under Articles 85 and 86 of the Treaty and the Merger Regulation.

Proposals of mergers fall under the jurisdiction of the Commission if they exceed a critical size. The Commission is in charge of investigating the merger as well as deciding whether it is to be accepted and under which conditions. Decisions can only be challenged in the Court of Justice; the Council has no right to overrule the decision of the Commission. The investigation procedure is conducted by the services of the Commission, namely by the Merger Task Force of the Competition Directorate General (DG IV) to which merger proposals have to be notified. The Merger Task Force receives the views of representatives of member states through the Advisory Committee on concentrations. It also has informal contacts with national administrations and with other parts of the Commission. Companies lobby through all these channels. Such decisions are not delegated to officials within the Commission, but are taken at the level of commissioners themselves by majority vote. While the views of the competition commissioner may typically carry a lot of weight, his or her voting power is no greater than that of any other commissioner.

As indicated by Neven *et al.* (1993), the problem with this procedure is its lack of transparency. Only a brief statement of reasons for the final decision is published, while the entire investigation procedure remains confidential. This provides opportunities for powerful firms with lobbying muscle to influence decisions. The absence of public debate and the need to publish no more than a bland *ex-post* rationalization of its decision make it less politically costly for the Commission to allow a dubious merger to go through.

5.3   Regulatory theory

It is often assumed that public authorities act as benevolent maximizers of the public interest. In contrast, economists such as Stigler (1971) have argued that government agencies cater for sectoral or other special interests of various kinds, such as a regulated industry itself ('capture'), their own bureaucracy, or the interests of a particular geographical area. This section summarizes the main ideas from the recent theoretical literature which will be used in the next section to discuss reform options for European institutions.

Such problems are best analysed in the context of a delegation process: citizens delegate general political power to their parliamentary representatives, who in turn delegate the regulatory power to potentially self-interested agencies (see, for example, Laffont and Tirole, 1993). Regulation then becomes a multi-tiered principal-agent problem: the industry is monitored by the agency, which in turn is monitored by the citizens' representatives. Controlling the agency becomes more difficult as the information advantages shared by the industry and the agency become greater. These information advantages open the way for potential collusion between the industry and the agency at the expense of the public.

These ideas lead to the conclusion that the regulatory process ought to be as transparent as possible to limit the potential for collusion between industry and the agency. While this recommendation sounds quite obvious, how such transparency is to be achieved is a more intriguing question. Political scientists such as McCubbins and Schwartz (1984) contrast *fire alarm* controls with *police patrols*. The latter are meant to represent centralized control, operating at the initiative of the legislature. The authors argue that this form of control is more expensive than 'fire alarms' – a set of procedures which are supposed to enable citizens and interest groups to trigger action if agencies or other parties threaten to violate the law. They stress that fire alarms are the dominant form of control in the United States, where Congress relies heavily on lobbying by organized groups to keep regulatory agencies on their toes. Moreover, Congress has set up specific 'advocates' to represent groups that find it relatively more difficult to be heard. The Departments of Agriculture, Labour, and Commerce do this for farmers, labour and small-business interests, respectively.[8]

A similar point is made by McCubbins *et al.* (1987), who stress the widespread use of administrative procedures as an *ex-ante* instrument of control and thus a complement to *ex-post* 'fire-alarm' monitoring. In the United States, the procedures used by federal agencies for rule-making are governed by the Administrative Procedure Act[9] which requires (quoting McCubbins *et al.*, 1987, pp. 257–8):

'1. The agency cannot announce a new policy without warning, but must instead give "notice" that it will consider an issue, and do so without prejudice or bias in favour of any particular action.

'2. Agencies must solicit "comments" and allow all interested parties to communicate their views.

'3. Agencies must allow "participation" in the decision-making process, with the extent often mandated by the organic statute creating the agency as well as by the courts (...). If hearings are held, then parties may be allowed to bring forth testimony and evidence and often to cross-examine other witnesses.

'4. Agencies must deal explicitly with the evidence presented to them and provide a rationalizable link between the evidence and their decisions.'

A lesson from this literature – and from the US experience with regulation – is that transparency can be achieved by giving an explicit voice to competing special interests who act as advocates of their own cause. It is, however, important to create a level playing field, that is, to ensure equal representation of all sides to the issue in an open and explicit procedure, as opposed to granting exclusive behind-the-scenes access to powerful insiders. For example, communication from interested parties to an agency engaged in rule-making is usually required to be placed in a file available for public inspection.

Apart from transparency, a vital issue is what incentives or 'missions' agencies should be given to ensure they pursue them forcefully instead of reluctantly. In an influential book, Wilson (1991) has argued that agencies with clear and simple missions often perform better than agencies with complex and contradictory missions. Dewatripont and Tirole (1995) show that it is hard to give agencies incentives to present the arguments for and against a policy equally forcefully, if the rewards they obtain are based on the enacted policy decision instead of the – admittedly harder to observe – quality of the arguments put forward. This suggests splitting tasks or missions between separate agencies.

These arguments can be illustrated by the case of merger control, where two questions typically arise: how does a proposed merger affect prices and thus consumer surplus, and how does it affect productive efficiency? It is interesting that the EC Merger Regulation singles out the first consideration as the 'mission' of the Commission. Theoretically, this conforms to the principle of giving an agency a clear, simple mission. In reality, the producer side of the argument is also forcefully put forward through intense lobbying, which seems able at least to re-establish the balance, if not more.

5.4　Improving enforcement

We have learned from the previous section – and in particular from the references to the US experience – that the reform of enforcement procedures should focus on *transparency* and *missions*. In this section we discuss some ideas for improving enforcement, first in relation to state aids and merger regulation, and second in relation to judicial procedures.

5.4.1　State aids and merger regulation

These two areas currently share a number of features. Official responsibility for decisions lies with the European Commission which is responsible for both investigating and deciding on the matter. Moreover, intense lobbying takes place behind the scenes and lack of transparency is a widespread complaint. Finally, *ex-post* judicial review is possible but time-consuming.

A possible reform in both areas would entail setting up two agencies independent from the Commission that would be responsible for acting as 'prosecutors' by initiating action, one against mergers detrimental to consumers, and one against state aids that distort competition. These 'advocates' would then present their case to the Commission against that of the firms proposing a merger, or of the member state proposing to grant the subsidy. The creation of advocates with simple and clear missions that would argue openly would level the playing field. The Commission would then be expected to take the role of an impartial judge whose objective is to apply the Community rules. Its decisions would still be subject to review by the European Court of Justice or the Court of First Instance.

In the context of the Merger Regulation, Neven *et al.* (1993) argue in favour of giving the investigative responsibility to an independent merger task force, leaving the final decision to the Commission. This differs from anti-trust practice in Germany, where the independent cartel office is responsible not only for the investigation but also for the making the decision, although its decision, if it opposes the proposed merger, may be overruled by the federal economics minister, for instance on efficiency grounds.[10]

There is a choice between two possible systems. In the first, independent agencies have the power of decision over the industrial policy dispute, subject to the possibility of being challenged in the Courts. In the second, the independent agencies simply help to level the playing field by acting as advocates on behalf of the interests of a particularly weak party – such as the consumer – or guaranteeing the transparency of the investigation, as in the idea of the merger task force.

Neven *et al.* (1993) argue in favour of leaving the decision-making power with the Commission. Provided that the investigation procedure is transparent and that an independent agency can openly and forcefully push its case, there are advantages in keeping the decision power at the level of the Commission. This institution could enjoy more democratic legitimacy while also pursuing supranational goals. We return to the issue of the mission and the legitimacy of the Commission in Chapter 7. Two important points, however, should not be overlooked. First, as we argued above, the role of the Commission should be complemented by independent agencies. Second, it is important that any reform to enhance the efficiency of the decision-making process should move towards more supranationality. It should certainly avoid 'renationalization' of these responsibilities. Nor should it involve vesting more decision-making power in the Council of Ministers.

5.4.2   Judicial procedures

As suggested in the previous section, it may be appropriate to apply the 'fire alarm' principle to the enforcement of Community legislation, encouraging EU citizens and organizations to initiate legal action against non-enforcement of Single Market legislation. Legal action by citizens and firms against a state or against another natural or legal person inside the EU could make an important contribution to the enforcement of such legislation. A top-down approach, using legislation to harmonize the national administration and enforcement of Community law, is likely to prove a lengthy and perhaps contentious process. On the other hand, judicial decisions – both by the European Court of Justice and by national courts – have been highly effective as a *bottom-up* mechanism for creating new rights and remedies for individuals. The *Francovich* decision discussed above and the recent ruling in the *Telesystem* case,[11] for example, can be expected to lead to an acceleration of the correct transposition of EC directives into national laws.

Four important steps can be taken to increase the use of citizen initiative to enforce EU legislation. A first, obvious but crucial measure is to increase the supply of information about individual rights under these procedures. The Commission or an agency should be given a mandate to publicize widely the rights Community law gives to EU citizens against their own state, against other EU states and against other natural or legal persons. As mentioned above, individuals can already submit complaints to the Commission with a view to its taking action under Article 169. They may also bring proceedings in national courts to defend their rights under Community law and, through Article 177, they have indirect access to the Court of Justice which is the final authority on what these rights are. There is, however, only limited public awareness of these possibilities and the costs – for instance of a procedure that gives access to the Court of Justice – are often high. Both factors combine to discourage individuals and firms from challenging another party by appealing to Community law.

The second step is to address the problem of 'free-riding' and the lack of incentives. Individuals who successfully bring proceedings to defend their rights under Community law may benefit others more than themselves. Moreover, the principles established may be of general application and the publicity generated makes others aware of the rights that they have. Thus there is a positive externality attached to individuals taking legal action to defend their rights under Community law. There may be a strong case, therefore, not only for more publicity, but also for subsidizing citizens who wish to appeal to Community law; for instance, by paying part of their legal expenses.

Openness is the third point. There is a big gap between the public scrutiny to which national administrations are subject – in the domestic press, in particular – and the quality and extent of scrutiny of the Commission. Action should be taken to make the acts of the Commission and other EU bodies more transparent and more accessible to individuals and the media. A possible reform is to adopt the Swedish legal principle that all documents received and issued by official bodies should be publicly available. Action should also be taken to make the Commission's officials more accountable. We will return to this point in Chapter 7.

Publicity and transparency are important but not enough. If the Commission decides not to pursue a case against a state under Article 169 – even if it is well founded – individuals who have complained have no access to judicial review. Even though individuals and companies may take action against EU institutions under Article 175 for failure to act, this possibility does not apply – so far – to the exercise of the Commission's discretion under Article 169. The fourth point is that this should be changed and the citizens' status as plaintiffs against the Commission should be formally recognized. The Commission should not be forced to pursue any complaint made by an EU citizen automatically. However, when it refuses to do so, the Commission should not only justify its decision, but citizens should also have access to the Court of Justice to contest the legality of such a decision.

If citizens' rights in enforcing EU legislation are to be strengthened, it is important at the same time to reinforce the effectiveness of the Commission in its enforcement role. In particular, the perceived role of commissioners as representatives of their states weakens the executive power of the Commission to enforce Community law. The reforms of EU institutions we discuss in Chapter 7 address this problem.

A more active use of the 'fire alarm' principle can only work if sanctions against violations of Single Market legislation are credible; that is, if people believe that they will be implemented. As mentioned above, there should be a consistent set of remedies and penalties in all the member states for violations of EC law by private parties. There is also a need for more effective sanctions against member states for breaches of Community law, including failure to enforce Community law against private parties. At present, there is no mechanism for enforcing payment by a state if a fine is imposed by the Court of Justice under Article 171. Possible sanctions include additional fines and temporary exclusion from the benefits of certain EU policies. Since the use of force is neither possible nor desirable, the gravest possible sanction would be the exclusion of a country from the EU. With enlargement, such a sanction would become more credible. It should, however, always be seen as the ultimate sanction and it should be applied only if it could be proved that a country was failing systematically to comply with the rules governing the common base.

Notes

1. Council Regulation (EEC) No. 4064/89 of 21 December 1989 on the control of concentrations between undertakings.

2. The regulation took effect in September 1990. Between this date and December 1994, 288 mergers were notified to the Commission. Only 17 decisions were the result of the thorough investigation procedure, the remainder being either withdrawn, ruled to be outside the scope of the regulation or, for the overwhelming majority of cases, cleared within a month. Of these 17 decisions, 5 were cleared without any conditions or obligations, 10 were cleared with conditions or obligations and 2 were prohibited.

3. CEC (1995a). The number of infringement procedures varies a great deal among member states. In 1994 there were fewer than 75 procedures against Denmark, Ireland, Luxembourg, the Netherlands and the United Kingdom, but more than 95 procedures against Greece, Italy and Portugal.

4. The Commission has published in the *Official Journal* a standard form for this purpose: OJ 1989 C 26/6.

5. *Francovich and Others v Italy*, Cases C–6/90, C–9/90, [1991] ECR–I–5357.

6. For more details about the public lack of knowledge of the European Court of Justice, see Gibson and Caldeira (1995).

7. See Directive 89/665, OJ L395/33 1989. Directive 92/13 (OJ L76/14 1992) deals with remedies in the field of utilities procurement. Procurement is an area of particular concern to the Commission which has announced that it intends to include specific penalty clauses in the regulations and directives it will issue.

8. The system of 'ombudsman', emanating from long-time practice in Sweden, relies on similar ideas.

9. 5 USC § 553. The Act dates originally from 1946. See Administrative Conference of the United States, *A Guide to Federal Agency Rulemaking*, Washington DC (2nd ed.) 1991.

10. The lack of such efficiency defence in the Merger Regulation is responsible for much of the lack of transparency in the decisions by the Commission. See Jacquemin (1990).

11. In January 1995 a Milan-based telecommunications services firm, Telesystem, challenged the Italian telephone monopoly, appealing to a directive not yet transposed into Italian law. The case was brought to a national court which ruled in favour of Telesystem, applying the principle that directives are effective even if the country has failed to transpose them.

6   Currency union and other open partnerships

6.1   Introduction

Flexible integration distinguishes policy areas that belong to the common base of the EU from those where cooperation should not be mandatory. Areas of cooperation outside the common base are the domain of open partnerships. The term 'partnerships' is appropriate, because participation is not compulsory for EU states as it is in the policy areas that belong to the common base. Partnerships are 'open' because there should be no discrimination among EU states: the same entry and exit rules must apply to all.

As argued in Chapter 3, allowing a *subset* of countries to cooperate in a specific policy dimension can make everybody better off. It is possible, however, that a partnership could interfere with the common base or impose a cost on those countries that do not participate in the agreement. Similarly, those states which decide not to cooperate in a given policy area could have an incentive to adopt policies that hurt the members of the partnership. When important externalities are present, the decision to set up an open partnership, the entry and exit rules, and the behaviour of non-members *vis-à-vis* members are all issues which should be carefully addressed *before* a group of countries goes ahead with cooperation in a particular policy area.

Assigning a policy area to an open partnership does not mean that cooperation will always be limited to a subset of EU states. On the contrary, experimentation and 'learning-by-doing' may be easier in a smaller group. Positive experience of states that cooperate in a specific area can create imitation effects, inducing others to join at a later stage. In this respect the history of the EMS is instructive. The EMS began in 1979, following a resolution of the European

Council. It was set up outside the Community institutions, however, through an agreement among the central banks of the member states.[1] Over time, the positive experience of those states that had joined the Exchange Rate Mechanism (ERM) of the EMS at the beginning – particularly their success in reducing the increase in unemployment produced by disinflationary policies – persuaded other member states to join.

Arrangements similar to open partnerships already exist, such as the Schengen agreement on border controls and the Western European Union (WEU). Such partnerships were set up outside the framework of the EU and thus outside any EU rules. This has the potential to create problems; Schengen is a case in point. The EU members of the Nordic Passport Union – Denmark, Sweden and Finland – wanted to extend the Schengen agreement to Norway, which is a member of the Nordic Passport Union but not of the EU. This particular question was resolved in favour of including Norway within Schengen, with the same obligations but with fewer rights than EU states. Other open partnerships outside the framework of the EU, however, may create problems that are much more difficult to resolve.

Policy dimensions as distinct as defence, the environment, or monetary policy – all of which could in principle be organized in open partnerships – raise quite different problems. It is probably undesirable – and certainly unfeasible – to write down specific rules that apply to all possible partnerships. Rules for open partnerships necessarily constitute incomplete contracts. As opposed to a complete contract, which specifies what decisions should be taken in the event of all possible future contingencies, an incomplete contract defines only who should decide and when, that is, it allocates the control or decision rights. Chapter 7 contains a further discussion of constitutional rules as incomplete contracts.

Open partnerships require three sets of control rights: first, the power to deal with the externalities that members and non-members may impose on one another; second, the power to decide the entry and exit rules; and third, the power to administer the partnership.

6.1.1 Dealing with the externalities

The rules for an open partnership should address the externalities that members and non-members of the partnership can impose on one another. When externalities are unimportant, states should be allowed to cooperate as they wish, but this is likely to be the exception. In the presence of externalities, the decision to set up a partnership and the interaction between members and non-members are matters of common interest to all EU states: those that wish to cooperate in this particular area and those that prefer to stay out.

Monetary policy is an example full of externalities. A strong argument suggests that competitive devaluations would disrupt the internal market – the essence of the common base of the EU. Assume that one group of states wishes to unify its monetary policies, possibly adopting a common currency. Can the others simply decide to maintain independent monetary policies? The case is not just theoretical. It reflects the situation created by the Maastricht approach to stage III of EMU. For many years only a subset of European states is likely to adopt a common currency. This will coexist with some, possibly many, independent currencies. The Treaty is silent, however, on the question of how to deal with the threat of competitive devaluations.

Environmental policies offer another example. Setting up an environmental partnership creates a free-rider problem, as in the example of Chapter 3 section 3.3. Members of the partnership adhere to strict environmental standards, while the countries outside pollute, but benefit from being close to 'clean' countries.

Common border controls – as in the Schengen agreement – are an example of negative externalities. If a few states decide to eliminate border controls among themselves, it is likely that controls *vis-à-vis* the outside world – including those EU states that are not members of Schengen – will become tougher. This may increase the pressure of illegal immigration on the non-members. Tougher controls may also cause extra inconvenience to citizens travelling between Schengen and non-Schengen states.

Cooperation in defence is another important example. At present ten EU states (Belgium, France, Germany, Greece, Italy,

Luxembourg, the Netherlands, Portugal, Spain and the United Kingdom) form a defence partnership, the Western European Union. Among the EU states that do not participate in the WEU, four are neutral: Sweden, Finland, Austria and Ireland. Although the Maastricht Treaty describes the WEU as 'an integral part of the development of the Union' (Article J.4.2), some current WEU members think it should remain distinct from the EU, because neutral states can hardly be expected to take part in operational discussions on defence. At the same time, smaller partnerships are forming within the WEU to deal with regional security problems; for example, the common land and sea forces recently created by France, Italy and Spain.

As noted in Chapter 3, defence partnerships can give rise to both positive and negative externalities (see sections 3.3.6–7). A free-rider problem arises since defence agreements among a subset of European states are likely to enhance the security of those that do not participate. But the defence partnership could also impose negative externalities on non-members, by damaging their economic or political interests in the rest of the world.

What this discussion suggests is not only that integration in some policy dimensions should be voluntary – a basic principle of flexible integration – but also that the externalities introduced by an open partnership are a common problem. The solution to such problems must, therefore, belong to the common base. The institutions that administer the common base should thus have decision-making power in all areas where the presence of an open partnership gives rise to important externalities. Such decisions should obviously be made before a subset of states is allowed to form a partnership.

For example, if a subset of the EU members decides to form a currency union, the rules to address the possible externalities of the monetary interactions between members and non-members must be obeyed by all states and must be monitored by an institution that belongs to the common base of the EU.

6.1.2   The entry rules

How should the entry rules into an open partnership be designed? The solution to this problem will never be easy. Partnerships should be open, not only in the sense that no state can be compelled to join, but also in the sense that every EU state has the right to join, if it meets the criteria set out in the entry rules. There must be no discrimination against particular member states. Furthermore, the entry criteria must have a rational basis and purpose; that is, they must not be a disguised form of discrimination. A corollary of the no-discrimination principle is that all Union states should have some say in what the entry rules are to be.

If all states can enter automatically, however – provided they satisfy some pre-announced criteria – the entry rules may end up being unnecessarily strict. Some Union members may insist on rules that protect them against entry by states that, once accepted in the partnership, may impose costs on the other members.

This bias could only be circumvented by avoiding pre-announced criteria and having an entry rule that allows the current members of a partnership to decide unilaterally whether or not to allow a new member to join. The ERM, for example, had no entry rules: any EC states could ask to join,[2] but the decision to accept a new country was left to the existing members. When the EMS was negotiated this veto power on the acceptance of new members made it much easier to come to an agreement. No complicated provisions had to be written to regulate the entry of new members or to regulate the working of the system in the event that an 'undesired' currency were to join. This tension – between entry rules that may be unnecessarily strict and a unilateral decision that allows for discrimination – cannot be easily resolved, but in each case some body will have to do it. As discussed further in section 7.2, it is appropriate to give decision rights over issues that involve political judgements to a political body like the Council.

6.1.3 The administration of open partnerships

We have already pointed out that the decision-making power over the externalities associated with the presence of an open partnership should rest with the institutions of the common base. Each partnership, however, will presumably require its own administration: who should provide it, and where should it be located? There are two models: all partnerships could be administered by the Commission; or each partnership could have its own bureau in one of the participating states. The first solution has the advantage of bringing all open partnerships into the 'European House' and can exploit economies of scale in administrative services. But it creates opportunities for free-riding; it also tends to downplay the separation between the supranational common base and the more intergovernmental partnerships. The second model makes that distinction very clear, but it forgoes administrative economies of scale, and creates a danger of too many dispersed activities. The desirable model depends on the type of partnership: for large ones the administration may be better handled by specialized bodies, like the European Central Bank, which *is not* a Community institution (in the sense of Article 4 TEU). Smaller partnerships could have administrations set up at the discretion of the participating states.

It is difficult to proceed further with this abstract discussion without reference to concrete examples. In the remainder of this chapter we analyse a specific example of an open partnership: a currency union. A currency union provides a good example of the issues that arise when we think about the rules of an open partnership: how to deal with the externalities, who has the power to decide the entry rules, how the partnership should be administered. In discussing a *monetary open partnership* we also wish to suggest that such an arrangement is preferable to the Maastricht construct of stage III of EMU. In particular, what the Maastricht Treaty already permits for some states – to opt out of the single currency – should be generalized to all states. All other aspects of the Treaty regarding EMU could be left unchanged.

6.2   Currency union

Article 105a of the Maastricht Treaty establishes the principle of a single currency: 'The ECB shall have the exclusive right to authorize the issue of bank notes within the Community.' For EU states other than Germany, the benefits of a single currency are mainly macroeconomic. For low-inflation states – France in particular – an important benefit is the ability to influence a European rather than Germany's monetary policy. For high-inflation states, the main benefit is to gain credibility for monetary policy. These benefits, however, exist only if Germany adopts the single currency. Although there could, hypothetically, be more than one currency union in the EU, the reality is that 'currency union' means currency union *with Germany*. A monetary union that did not include Germany would be meaningless, because the Deutschmark (DM) is the reserve currency, and the Bundesbank has the greatest credibility among European central banks. This immediately raises the following question: why should Germany accept giving up the DM?

6.2.1 Why Germany cares about the stability of intra-European exchange rates

Since the late 1960s German policy-makers have sought a coordinated response by European countries to the breakdown of the Bretton Woods system of fixed exchange rates. As it became clear that Bretton Woods was approaching its final days, German policy-makers became increasingly worried that other European states might not be able to follow the appreciation of the DM *vis-à-vis* the dollar, and that the subsequent realignments of intra-European parities would disrupt the European customs union. In the event, the decline of the dollar in the early 1970s led the DM to appreciate against both the dollar and the currencies of its European partners. The result was a large swing in Germany's terms of trade. From November 1969 to March 1973 the DM appreciated by 30% *vis-à-vis* the dollar. This was accompanied by a 17% worsening of Germany's overall competitiveness; a loss of competitiveness of 0.56% for each increase of 1% in the dollar-DM parity. A significant fraction of this relative price change derived from the change in Germany's terms of trade with its European partners. This experience helped shape German attitudes towards the plans, in the late 1970s, to recreate in Europe a small Bretton Woods System.[3]

From January 1985 to December 1987 the DM appreciated 100.3% against the dollar. This time the overall loss of competitiveness was 33.5% – only 0.33% for each increase of 1% in the dollar-DM parity; that is, half the amount experienced in the 1969–73 episode. The reason for the greater stability is that EMS currencies followed the DM much more closely, thus weakening the impact of the dollar's fall on Germany's terms of trade. After the EMS crisis of September 1992, however, the situation seems to have reverted to that of the pre-EMS period. Between June and December 1994 the DM appreciated 12.4% *vis-à-vis* the dollar, and each percentage

Table 6.1 The volatility of Germany's terms of trade (monthly data)

	Standard deviation of the real effective exchange rate (global index)	Correlation between the global and the intra-ERM indices of competitiveness
January 1972–January 1979	0.0464	0.7393
February 1979–August 1992	0.1081	–0.4543
September 1992–December 1994	0.0254	0.3726

Definitions: Real exchange rates are constructed using producer prices, except for the Netherlands, Switzerland, the United Kingdom and Germany, where we used wholesale prices, and France where we used consumer prices for lack of better data. Effective real exchange rates are computed as arithmetic averages of bilateral rates using the IMF–MERM weights for 1977 normalized to cover only Germany's eight major trading partners: Belgium (0.0588 in the global index, 0.121 in the intra-ERM index), France (0.2016 and 0.416), Italy (0.151 and 0.311), the Netherlands (0.074 and 0.152), the United Kingdom (0.058), Japan (0.152), the United States (0.262), Switzerland (0.043). The United Kingdom was not included in the intra-ERM index because the pound belonged to the mechanism only for a very short period.
Sources: IMF, *International Financial Statistics* and OECD, *Main Economic Indicators*.

point of appreciation produced a fall in Germany's overall competitiveness of 0.58%, larger than in the early 1970s.[4]

The role of the EMS in stabilising Germany's terms of trade is evident even when considering the short-term variability of the real effective exchange rate, rather than its long-term swings. We have constructed the real effective exchange rate of the DM *vis-à-vis* its main ERM partners,[5] and we have computed the correlation between an index of 'global' competitiveness and another index of Germany's competitiveness inside the ERM. The numbers are shown in Table 6.1. In the 1970s the correlation between the two indexes was very high, indicating that the French franc, the lira and the other European currencies did not follow the DM in its large appreciation against the dollar after the collapse of Bretton Woods. The phenomenon reverses between 1979 and 1992: the correlation between the global index and the intra-ERM index becomes negative, indicating that the ERM dampened the fluctuations in Germany's competitiveness. After September 1992, when the ERM was disrupted, the correlation turns positive again, which is an indication of the importance of Italy in total German trade.

6.2.2   The politics of Maastricht

Observing that Germany cares about the stability of intra-European exchange rates is a big step away from concluding that Germany has a macroeconomic incentive to join a European currency union. A single European currency would eliminate the variability of intra-European exchange rates by definition, but at a high cost for Germany. During the 1980s Germany *de facto* ran European monetary policy with almost no constraints from other European countries. It also achieved credibility, low inflation and, as we have seen, significant stability in its terms of trade. Returning to a system that dampens intra-European exchange rate variability would clearly benefit Germany. This does not require moving all the way to abandoning the DM, however.

Germany's incentives to give up the DM are ultimately not economic but political (Fratianni and von Hagen, 1992). A single currency would certainly foster further political integration in Europe. That, in turn, could make it more likely that one day there will be a common European foreign policy, which is something Germany seems to value a great deal, because of both its history and its location at the boundary between Western and Eastern Europe. The benefits of a single currency for other EU states are mainly macroeconomic, but depend entirely on Germany's participation. This strong element of asymmetry in the distribution of the economic gains from adopting a single currency gives Germany a lot of bargaining power in the design of European monetary arrangements.

There is also an important zero-sum element to the gains from adopting a single currency. Low-inflation states would benefit mainly from gaining influence over German monetary policy. Naturally, this is a loss to Germany. For the high-inflation countries, the main benefit would be to gain credibility. But if high inflation in such countries is a political problem, that is, it reflects popular attitudes towards inflation or malfunctioning political institutions, their increased credibility could come at the expense of Germany, which would see its credibility diminished. Thus the costs of a single currency for Germany increase with the number of high-inflation countries that adopt it, both because its voting powers are diluted and because its credibility may be affected.

These considerations profoundly influenced the Maastricht design of the single European currency. This is most obvious in three areas: the rules for entry to the currency union, the design of the European Central Bank and the relations between the states that adopt the single currency and those that do not – either because they opt out, or because they fail to meet the entry criteria and so have a derogation. We address each of these points in the next three sections.

The entry rules

The Maastricht Treaty laid down detailed rules for the right to adopt the single currency based on four 'convergence criteria':

(i) A member state must not be the subject to a Council decision that it has an 'excessive deficit'. Such decisions result from the Excessive Deficit Procedure of Article 104c which operates as follows. The Commission monitors compliance with budgetary discipline on the basis of two reference values: an annual budget deficit of 3% of GDP, and a debt-to-GDP ratio of 60%. If the debt-to-GDP ratio is exceeded the Commission must make a report, unless it decides that the ratio is 'sufficiently diminishing' and 'approaching the reference value at a satisfactory pace'. If the budget deficit exceeds 3% the Commission must make a report unless either 'the ratio has declined substantially and continuously and reached a level that comes close to the reference value' or 'the excess over the reference value is only exceptional and temporary and the ratio remains close to the reference value'. If the Commission thinks that a state does not fulfil the requirements under one or both of the criteria, it must prepare a report which takes into account not only the reference values, but also whether the government deficit exceeds government investment expenditure and other relevant factors, including the medium-term economic and budgetary position of the member state. The final decision that a state has an excessive deficit lies with Ecofin,[6] which makes 'an overall assessment'. Factors relevant to this assessment are not specified in the Treaty.

(ii) The inflation rate must not exceed by more than 1.5% the rate in the three member states that perform best in terms of price stability.

(iii) The exchange rate must, for at least two years and without severe tensions, have stayed within the 'normal fluctuation margins provided for the Exchange Rate Mechanism of the EMS. In particular, the member state shall not have devalued its currency's bilateral central rate against any other currency on its own initiative for the same period'.

(iv) Long-term interest rates on average, during the previous year, should not have exceeded by more than 2% those in the three member states that perform best in terms of price stability.

The first of the four criteria is discretionary. The Council, meeting in the composition of the heads of state or of government will decide, acting by a qualified majority on the basis of the recommendations by Ecofin, which member states fulfil the necessary conditions to adopt a single currency. At that stage, the numbers written in the Treaty and Protocols will be very helpful in deflecting claims that anything other than rational economic criteria are being used to exclude some states from the currency union.[7] The decision, however, will not be an easy one, as is evident from discussions about what to do with Belgium. It is apparent that Belgium, despite having the highest debt-to-GDP ratio in the EU (140%), belongs to the *Greater DM area*; at least this is the view of financial markets, as reflected in long-term interest rates. The yield differential between ten-year German government bonds and ten-year bonds issued by Belgium is around 50 basis points. This compares with a yield differential in excess of 400 basis points for Italy and Spain, both of which have a lower debt-to-GDP ratio.

Understanding why the Treaty negotiators opted for rigid entry rules is important to understand the compromises that are likely to accompany the creation of open partnerships. The rules for entry to the currency union, as laid out by the convergence criteria, find very weak support in economic or constitutional analysis. The long transition period before the currency union begins and the decision to base the convergence criteria on quantitative reference values make little economic sense, as shown by our discussion of

Belgium. Entering the precise reference values into a protocol to the Treaty, thus giving them constitutional status, is also at odds with what should normally belong to a constitutional text. As some national delegations argued during the Maastricht negotiations, the numeric values should have been left to Community legislation.[8] At the same time, however, the Treaty leaves substantial discretion in the interpretation of the convergence criteria, so that – in the end – the decision on which states to admit will be essentially political.

The concerns of the German delegation, worrying about the prospect of a loss in monetary sovereignty, thus resulted in a text full of *road-blocks*. On paper these make the entry to the currency union extremely difficult. Since each road-block requires the exercise of judgement and is subject to interpretation, however, the decision about whom to admit will involve difficult negotiations, in which Germany will *de facto* have veto power. It should be noted in this context that the two chambers of the German parliament (Bundestag and Bundesrat) accompanied their approval of the Maastricht Treaty with a resolution requiring the German government to obtain their approval before accepting – in the European Council – to give up the DM. The precise legal effects of the resolution may be disputed, but the political intention is abundantly clear: it is a *do-it-yourself* opt-out provision to prevent the Council applying the convergence criteria too leniently.[9]

A large German influence on the design of any monetary union flows naturally from the way in which the gains from a single currency are distributed across countries. As already remarked, the peculiarity of Germany in any European monetary arrangement gives the country a lot of bargaining power. It could be argued that it might have been more efficient to acknowledge from the start the peculiarity of Germany and grant explicitly and *de jure* the veto powers that it has *de facto*. In this way the long and excruciating transition phase could have been avoided, and thus the accompanying danger of destabilizing speculative attacks. This is how the EMS worked: entry into the ERM had to be unanimously approved by all existing members. But these veto powers did not prevent the system from growing over time to include almost all European states.

A currency union, however, is very different from a system of fixed-but-adjustable parities: there is no explicit provision for exit, and the costs to Germany of letting in a high-inflation country are larger. If entry had to be approved by all existing members, the currency union could exclude some states indefinitely, simply because they would diminish the benefits of the single currency for those already in it.

This discussion does not solve the lack of economic and constitutional justification for the Maastricht criteria, but it explains why they were adopted. Granting Germany veto power and forgetting about the entry criteria might have been more efficient, but it would have violated the principle of non-discrimination. Hence the compromise: precise entry criteria to deflect the criticism of unilateral discrimination, but *unnecessarily rigid* rules to accommodate the low-inflation states worrying about high-inflation states joining the monetary union.

These criteria are unlikely to be easily improved, precisely because they were the result of a difficult compromise. In our opinion, they could still apply for those states that wish to go ahead with a single currency. Moreover, the Maastricht timetable has already affected policy decisions and market expectations as reflected, for example, in interest rates and long-term bond prices. The timetable spelled out in the Maastricht Treaty, therefore, should not be changed for the same group of countries.

The European Central Bank

Similar observations can be made about the European Central Bank (ECB). The institutional design of the ECB reflects that of the Bundesbank, with the addition that the ECB's independence has explicit constitutional protection in the Treaty. The ECB is likely to be different from the Bundesbank in its accountability and legitimacy, as well as in its attitude on rules versus discretion in monetary policy.

Rules versus discretion. The reputation of a central bank is a crucial factor in choosing a point along the trade-off between rules and discretion in monetary policy. An institution that enjoys a high reputation can use discretion. A central bank that does not enjoy a similar reputation must look for credibility through binding itself by rigid rules. The ECB will be a new institution with no track record. In order to build a reputation it will have to follow strict rules and – at least for some time – allow itself very little discretion. Building a reputation is likely to take much longer than it took for the Bundesbank because, elsewhere in Europe, attitudes towards inflation have not been shaped by a common experience. The states that emerged from the collapse of the Austrian empire at the end of the first world war (Germany, Austria, Czechoslovakia and Hungary) experienced, in the 1920s, a hyperinflation followed by a monetary reform. In Germany the hyperinflation was ultimately linked to the collapse of its democratic institutions, and these events have become part of German memory. Nothing similar happened in the United Kingdom, France or Italy.

Thanks to its reputation, the Bundesbank has at times been able to run monetary policy with flexibility and *good common sense*. For example, in 1989 the Bundesbank accommodated the sharp increase in money demand[10] which followed the flight out of government bonds after the announcement that a withholding tax would be introduced. In fact, there is no systematic evidence that the Bundesbank refrains from engaging in stabilization policies to a greater extent than most other central banks, or that the volatility of German output is significantly higher than in other industrial states.

Accountability and legitimacy. The German public's preference for low inflation gives the Bundesbank a degree of popular legitimacy on its own account which limits the pay-off politicians can expect from threatening its independence (see Lohmann, 1994). This is unlikely to be the case for the ECB, particularly if there are significant variations in the policy preferences of different European governments and their electorates. The framers of the Treaty aimed to make the ECB legitimate by assigning it a constitutionally entrenched obligation to give absolute priority to price stability[11] and by requiring it to make its activities transparent through regular reporting (Article 109b). *Price stability* is not defined by the Treaty, however, nor is there any requirement for the ECB to define what it understands by price stability. Moreover, because EU institutions are a mixture of supranational and intergovernmental bodies it is difficult to identify a *principal* on whose behalf the ECB can act, leaving it exposed to accusations that it is a body accountable to no one.

One way around this problem is to ask the ECB to pursue its goal of price stability by publicly announcing an *inflation target* and publishing regular inflation reports. The European Monetary

Institute (EMI) – which is responsible for preparing stage III of EMU – has not yet taken a view on a desirable monetary strategy for the ECB. The EMI president recognizes that transparency and accountability are the criteria that should govern the choice of a strategy for the ECB, but concludes that both monetary targeting and inflation targeting satisfy these criteria (see Lamfalussy, 1995). The instability of the demand for money and the lack of experience with EU-wide monetary aggregates, however, suggests that transparency and accountability will be better served by an inflation target.[12][13]

Who should set the inflation target for the ECB? The experience of the countries which have adopted inflation targets suggests that it is desirable that inflation targets be mutually acceptable to the government and the central bank (see section 6.3). The ECB should thus coordinate its inflation target with Ecofin, or, better, with the Ecofin members representing the states that have adopted the single currency. Once again, however, the fuzzy institutional design of the EU could make such coordination difficult. The Council is an intergovernmental body with a dispersion of different views.[14] An alternative and perhaps more workable solution is to leave the choice of the target to the bank, whose proposal would in any case carry the day if faced with a divided Ecofin.

The relation between the common currency and the other EU currencies. The convergence criteria and the problems of the ECB are not the only weak points in the Maastricht blueprint of stage III of EMU. As we have seen, the entry rules give Germany a *de facto* veto power to delay the entry of weak currencies. There are also some currencies – the pound sterling, and the Danish and Swedish krone – that may not join even if Germany were to accept them. But the Treaty, while creating the conditions for a lengthy period of coexistence of the common currency and the national monies of states outside the currency union, is silent on the question of how to coordinate monetary and exchange rate policy between the single currency group and the others. This issue is – or should be – at the centre of today's policy debate.

6.3　Rules for monetary coexistence in the EU

The upshot of the preceding analysis is that the Maastricht Treaty has *de facto* created an open monetary partnership. In this section we address the externalities that arise between the members of the monetary partnership and the states that do not adopt the common currency. As argued above, the mechanisms to deal with these externalities belong to the common base of the EU, and should be administered by the institutions of the common base.

We interpret our discussion of the common currency as an example of how to build and run an open partnership. But the arguments, and our specific proposal, apply even if the reader wishes to think of the current provisions for stage III of EMU as an instance of the multispeed approach to integration. The important policy problem is how to organize the coexistence, inside the EU, of a partnership with a common currency and many other countries with independent currencies. This problem remains independently of the way we think about the future of European economic integration. It is a problem, and the Treaty provides no guidance for the solution.

There are several arguments in favour of some coordination of monetary policy between the ECB and the EU central banks of states that – perhaps temporarily – do not adopt the single currency. Two of these arguments, in our view, are particularly compelling. First, the countries outside the currency union are likely to be precisely those where public opinion is relatively less concerned with inflation. Policy-makers in such states will thus have an incentive to use the exchange rate as an instrument to control aggregate demand, that is, to engage in competitive devaluations. Second, in some states outside the currency union the public finance position may become – at least in the eyes of financial markets – unsustainable. In the event of a financial crisis *Tequila effects* – so-called after the Mexican crisis which affected financial institutions throughout the United States – may impinge on the Union's members. The consequences of financial bankruptcies in one country may spread to financial intermediaries abroad. The ECB may find itself in the difficult position of having to choose between providing liquidity to the financial system, or sticking to its target and risking further bankruptcies.

Both effects – competitive devaluations and cross-border transmission of financial crises – are good illustrations of the externalities that may arise between the members of a given partnership (in this case the monetary union partnership) and the other states.

We discussed competitive devaluations in section 4.5. We concluded that attempts to increase competitiveness *per se* are not necessarily undesirable. On the contrary, they may stimulate productivity and efficiency. What should be avoided are attempts to improve competitiveness through the discretionary use of monetary policy. Mechanisms that prevent member states from doing so should thus be part of the common base of EU policies; that is, no member state should be allowed to opt out. A specific proposal in this regard is presented next.

6.3.1   Inflation targets

How can we ensure that both groups of states – those adopting the common currency and those outside – will not use monetary policy to produce temporary gains in competitiveness? One solution – suggested by Alexandre Lamfalussy, President of the EMI – is to create a new ERM with the common currency at the centre and the other currencies fluctuating within bands. But this idea would not work. The ERM survived for 13 years under two very special conditions: controls on capital movements and compulsory central bank intervention in the foreign exchange markets. Capital controls in many European countries – Spain and Italy in particular – lasted until the late 1980s. Compulsory intervention by the Bundesbank when the bilateral rate between the DM and any other currency in the mechanism reached the limits of the band was the rule, or at least currency markets anticipated this to be the rule. None of these conditions would hold in an exchange rate agreement between the ECB and the central banks of states that do not adopt the common currency. Restrictions on the movement of capital are ruled out by the Single Market. Automatic intervention by the ECB would undermine its commitment to price stability, as the Bundesbank consistently argued throughout the life of the ERM.

An alternative is to follow a suggestion made by Mervyn King of the Bank of England: the central banks of all EU states – those that adopt the common currency and those that do not – should commit to inflation targets. Inflation targets thus become part of the common base. Failure to adopt them would be tantamount to breaking a rule of the Single Market, such as the refusal to eliminate a non-tariff barrier.[15]

Inflation targets for all EU states – beyond being desirable in themselves – have two specific advantages. First, they reinforce the commitment to low inflation, making monetary policy dominant with regard to fiscal policy, a ranking that is particularly important in countries where an unsustainable fiscal situation creates the incentive to use inflation as a fiscal tool.

Second, attempts to engineer a competitive devaluation would either become impossible – if the central bank delivers on its commitment to the target – or be frustrated by the market's reaction to a failure to meet the inflation target. This obviously requires transparency in monitoring the targets of individual states, a point to which we return later. Inflation targets will reduce the volatility of *nominal* exchange rates, but some variability – not related to market fundamentals – will remain. Long-term swings in *real exchange rates*, that is, misalignments such as those discussed in section 6.2.1 will, however, be significantly dampened.

Two questions arise. Who should set the targets? Who should monitor the inflation performance once a target has been set? Let us first consider the position of states that do not adopt the common currency.

Inflation targets for a state that has not adopted the common currency could be set independently by the state itself, by the state in consultation with the ECB, or possibly by Ecofin. Delegation becomes more desirable the more likely a state, left to decide on its own, would be to set the inflation target with the objective of inducing a competitive devaluation. We believe that this is an unlikely outcome since the stronger is the weight of the central bank in setting the target, the longer is the time horizon over which the target is announced. Moreover, if the central bank of a member state were to announce an unreasonably high inflation target, expectations – both in financial markets and in goods markets – would immediately respond to the announcement. Thus it is unlikely that the real exchange rate could be significantly affected, except perhaps in the very short run. We thus conclude that the decision about the targets can be left to the individual states, which may possibly result in different targets being chosen across the EU.

Who should decide inside each state? The experience of the countries that have adopted inflation targets is varied.[16] In New Zealand, the inflation target is part of a contract between the government and the central bank. In Sweden and Finland, the target is set independently by the central bank. In Canada, it is agreed between the government and the bank. It is probably desirable that inflation targets are agreed between the government and the central bank. A government continuously makes inflation announcements: when it tables the budget, when it signs public-sector wage contracts, when it sets the price of public services, and so on. It is advisable to avoid conflicting signals between the government's announcements and those that come from the central bank. Moreover, a target that is jointly announced by the government and the bank puts more responsibility upon the bank: it will not be able to justify a deviation from the target simply by shifting the blame to the government.

Even though the procedure for setting the target may be controversial, there should be no doubt about monitoring. The credibility of the inflation targets announced by a state that has not adopted the common currency should be enhanced by its participation in the European System of Central Banks (ESCB), which is already provided for by the Maastricht Treaty. Monitoring the individual targets should be delegated to the ESCB.[17] Such an arrangement would make it clear that even for those states that have not joined the common currency, the commitment to the inflation target is a duty owed not just to the domestic public and the national legislature, but also to the EU.

As already mentioned, commitment to an inflation target monitored by the ESCB should be part of the common base of the EU. No state could refuse to adopt an inflation target unless it left the EU. Blatant failure to meet the target must therefore carry some penalties. The Treaty already provides for sanctions in the case of excessive deficits, but only in stage III of EMU (Article 104c (11)). Penalties for failing to meet an inflation target could follow similar procedures.

6.3.2   Prudential regulation

For states such as Italy and Greece, where high inflation and weak currencies reflect fiscal rather than monetary problems, inflation targets may not be enough to make monetary policy dominant over fiscal policy, at least in the eyes of the markets. Tight money and low inflation raise the risk of a debt default. Will the ECB insist on imposing tight money on a country that is running a serious risk of financial collapse? The probable answer is no. When faced with the risk of a default that may spread to financial institutions throughout the Union, even the ECB will view inflation as a better solution to the financial crisis. Inflation targets are not credible in high-debt countries, even if the central bank is closely monitored by the ECB.

A devaluation induced by a fiscal problem, however, will rapidly translate into higher inflation: the competitiveness gain will be short-lived. In this sense the externality imposed on the other states will be small.[18]

There remains the risk that financial distress in a member state may spread to other states in the Union and undermine the credibility of their inflation targets. One way to cope with this problem is through ceilings on the ratios of public debt-to-assets for commercial banks throughout the EU. A previous MEI Report (Begg *et al.*, 1991) proposed two solutions to this problem. First, commercial banks should continuously compute the value of their assets using current market prices to value the government bonds they hold. Second, regulators, in assessing the solvency of a bank – or in computing Cooke ratios, that is, the allowed ratio of a bank's liabilities to its assets – should weigh government bonds owned by the bank according to the financial stability of the issuing institution. The latter could be assessed by an independent agency as in the case of private firms.

6.4   Conclusion

The Maastricht Treaty was a compromise between two opposing concepts of monetary union. The first was to assume that, sooner or later, all states would adopt the single currency. The second was to insist that high-inflation or high-debt countries should not become part of the monetary union since, if they did, monetary policy would lose credibility. The result of the compromise was a treaty that lays out detailed entry rules, but that *de facto* gives veto power to Germany without explicitly saying so. One unfortunate consequence of this arrangement is a lengthy and uncertain transition process, which can easily fall victim to speculative attacks.

We have argued that the holistic concept of stage III of EMU should be abandoned. Currency union should be treated as an open partnership, accepting from the start that only a subset of states are ready to go ahead in the foreseeable future. Accepting that not all states may adopt the common currency points immediately to the problem of how to coordinate policy between outsiders and insiders. We have advanced a solution to this problem: namely, that all European states announce and pursue inflation targets, and the ESCB monitors each country's performance against the announced targets. This solution would make it difficult to engage in competitive devaluations and would stabilize expectations. At the same time it would preserve some autonomy in national monetary policies to deal with country-specific shocks.

Notes

1. Resolution of the European Council of 5 December 1978; Agreement of 13 March 1979 between the central banks of the EEC, published in *Compendium of Community Monetary Texts*, Luxembourg, Office for Official Publications of the European Communities.

2. In fact all EC countries have been members of the EMS since the beginning. Only some, however, participated in the ERM. For those that were members of the EMS, but not of the ERM, membership was little more than a formality. But it established the important principle that everyone had the right to be considered as a potential member of the ERM.

3. For a discussion of the effects of that experience on German attitudes with regard to the EMS see Giavazzi and Giovannini (1989).

4. Data from Datastream Inc. and OECD, *Main Economic Indicators*; see also the footnote to Table 6.1.

5. The real effective exchange rate used to construct Table 6.1 covers only Germany's eight major trading partners, and within the ERM only Belgium, France, the Netherlands and Italy. Thus the difference in results following September 1992 is entirely attributable to the devaluation of the lira, since neither Belgium, nor France, nor the Netherlands devalued *vis-à-vis* the DM.

6. That is the Council, meeting in the composition of economic and finance ministers.

7. De Grauwe (1994) offers a similar interpretation of the convergence criteria.

8. The numbers can in theory be changed by unanimous Council decision (see Article 6 of the Protocol on the convergence criteria and Article 104c (14)) but there is a considerable *status quo* bias against such change.

9. The parliamentary resolutions and the finance minister's reply were considered by the German constitutional court in cases 2BvR 21344/92 and 2159/92. The court's judgement is published in English as *Brunner v European Union Treaty* [1994] 1 Common Market Law Reports 57.

10. The shift into money reached DM 25 billion in a single month.

11. Articles 3a, 105 EC. The requirement that the ESCB shall 'support the general economic policies in the Community' is expressed to be without prejudice to the goal of price stability. (Precisely *whose* policies the ESCB is supposed to support is not made clear.)

12. For a discussion of inflation targets see Persson and Tabellini (1993) and the readings in Leiderman and Svensson (1995).

13. von Hagen (1995) argues that despite common perceptions the Bundesbank also sets monetary policy on the basis of an inflation target.

14. See Alesina and Grilli (1992) for a good discussion of the monetary politics in a European central bank.

15. As noted previously, the Maastricht Treaty did not deal with the monetary coordination problem. Its institutional design, however, contains a number of features that constrain how such coordination could be organized. The proposal developed here is not entirely compatible with those constraints.

16. See the papers in Leiderman and Svensson (1995).

17. A related issue is the reliability of price data. This another area where all states should commit to a common standard, so that there is no risk that a country may 'play around' with the definition of inflation. A step in this direction is the recent Council regulation on the harmonization of CPI indexes.

18. The experience of the Italian lira after the devaluation of September 1992 is revealing. Initially the devaluation was not

followed by a corresponding increase in inflation and inflation expectations. The resulting gain in competitiveness simply matched the losses incurred by Italy since the previous EMS realignment (in January 1987). Later, however, when, partly because of political instability, the lira fell again (in the winter and spring of 1995) the devaluation was accompanied (and partly caused) by renewed worries about the sustainability of Italy's public debt and about the ability of the Italian Treasury to roll over the debt. On that occasion, contrary to the 1992 episode, inflation expectations – and inflation itself – reacted rapidly to the devaluation.

7 Reforming the European constitution

7.1   Points of departure

Legitimate political authority is defined by a constitution setting out the structure, powers and duties of various government bodies. The EU is not a state, nor is it certain that it will become one. European institutions exercise political authority, however, because Community law is binding on both member states and individuals. The constitutional basis of this authority is not set out in a document called *constitution*. It is embodied in the Treaties, in decisions of the Court of Justice and in customs and practices that have evolved over time.

Political constitutions are typical examples of *incomplete contracts*. A complete contract would define what decisions should be taken in the event of all possible future contingencies. In the hypothetical world of complete contracts, questions about the allocation and division of powers would not arise, since the constitution would have defined in advance all decisions to be taken. Even the task of checking on administrative implementation of decisions would have been taken care of by defining adequate incentive schemes. In such a world discussing the transfer of power between given government bodies is hardly meaningful.

In the real world, contracts are incomplete and, therefore, define allocations of *control rights*, that is, the rights of various parties to make decisions in given circumstances without defining what these decisions should be (see Grossman and Hart, 1986; and Hart, 1995). Political constitutions typify incomplete contracts since their main purpose is to define an allocation of powers, or decision rights in various domains. Constitutions typically partition domains of collective decision-making among various government institutions; they also specify choice procedures inside these institutions. Because constitutions are incomplete contracts, however, substantial discretionary power is left to various political and judicial institutions: the legislature, the executive and the courts. These discretionary powers could easily be abused unless they were limited by checks and balances, such as the separation of powers, designed to limit the power of given institutions to strictly defined areas and to counterbalance the power of one institution with that of another.[1]

Political constitutions ideally secure three objectives: adequate representation of different interests, especially protection of various minority rights; efficacy and adaptability in decision-making; and accountability of public officials and collective bodies responsible for policy decisions. Constitutional design entails both mutual support and subtle trade-offs among these three objectives.

Constitutions must protect the rights of minorities. In Europe, this applies especially to the rights of the individual member states. The strongest form of protection, used for some decisions in the Council of Ministers, is unanimity voting. Checks and balances in the relationships among the Council, the Commission and the European Parliament, access to the European Court of Justice, and requirements that certain decisions be approved in accordance with individual states' own constitutional procedures also serve the same purpose.

Efficacy and adaptability require political decision-making to be responsive to the wishes of majorities. This means both that majorities should be adequately represented and that agenda-setting powers should be conferred on appropriate bodies. By efficacy in decision-making, we mean avoiding gridlock or paralysis. By adaptability, we mean the ability to handle new and unforeseen events.

There is an obvious trade-off between efficacy and protecting the rights of individual states. Efficacy is sharply curtailed if a single state can veto a change that is very beneficial to all the others. Suppose, for example, that institutions at the Union level were deprived of agenda-setting powers, that is, exclusive or special rights to propose new laws. This would maximize the ability of an individual state to protect its position by submitting amendments to any new proposal. But if every state can submit amendments, which in turn are challenged by counter-amendments, and so on, the eventual result would be paralysis of decision-making. The quality of decision-making will also suffer from insufficient technical expertise or from procedures unduly responsive to short-term pressures. In many cases, appropriate institutional structures involve delegation. For example, a desirable feature of the Maastricht arrangements for a single currency is that monetary policy is delegated to the European Central Bank, rather than being the province of a political body such as the Council or the Parliament.

Accountability is needed to ensure that agents of specialized bodies do not pursue their own agendas, become captured by special interests or act corruptly.[2] Adequate representation of majority and minority interests requires democratic accountability mechanisms. Democratic accountability works best when the number of layers of delegation is small, for example by making individual decision-makers subject to election or to confirmation by the European Parliament. Accountability is also fostered by the possibility of judicial review of decisions, by eliminating monopoly rights to initiate legislation, and by opening up decision-making to public scrutiny and prior public comment. An important aspect of accountability is transparency, which refers to the ease with which citizens can gather usable information about the decision-making process and its results. Transparency thus requires not just that information should be available, but also that structures of decision-making should be easy to understand. Once again there is a trade-off between accountability and efficacy. Frequent elections and use of direct democracy may increase accountability at the price of a loss of efficacy.

To create legitimacy for political institutions in the eyes of the public, it is crucial to find an appropriate balance of protection, efficacy and accountability. This task is difficult, because the trade-offs among the three dimensions shift with the type of decision. Protection of minority rights is of overriding concern in decisions on constitutional change, whereas efficacy matters more in the normal exercise of power.

European institutions have two important weaknesses. First, decision-making inside the EU lacks efficiency. Stringent majority or unanimity requirements in the Council create a bias in favour of the *status quo*. Inefficiency is bound to worsen with enlargement, because there would be more countries with veto rights and because country interests would be more likely to diverge. Second, the intergovernmental mode of decision-making deprives citizens of information and control over Council decisions. Their control over the behaviour of the Commissioners – who are nominated by the national governments – is even smaller. Moreover, in their decisions in the Council, national governments probably care more about the majority interests that support them at home than about the interests of their domestic political opposition. This lack of accountability and imperfect representation is often referred to as the *democratic deficit* in Europe.

These weaknesses result from the hybrid nature of the present institutions, which seek to accommodate both federalist – supranational – and anti-federalist – intergovernmental – aspirations in a single structure. This leads to a third weakness: a fuzzy division of responsibility between different EU bodies and between EU bodies and national legislatures. By distinguishing the common base – in which integration is deeper and more supranational – from open partnerships which, from the Union's perspective, operate in the intergovernmental mode, flexible integration offers a more satisfactory and transparent way for the Union to accommodate both sets of aspirations. The next section considers how the relationship between the common base and the open partnerships might be organized and discusses arrangements to change the European Constitution. Section 7.3 reviews current decision-making in the EU and whether it is satisfactory for the common base. Section 7.4 discusses alternative reforms. Section 7.5 concludes.

7.2   The constitutional framework of flexible integration

A European Union based on flexible integration would have to satisfy two fundamental constitutional elements. The first consists of principles applicable to the relationship between the common base and the open partnerships. These include the principles that the – Union-wide – supranational mode of integration is limited to the policy areas included in the common base; and that new open partnerships should not interfere with the effective operation of the common base. The second element consists of the main principles of the common base itself. Prominent among these are the four freedoms – incorporating, as discussed in Chapter 4, the current content of Union citizenship – and respect for basic principles such as human rights, democratic government, the rule of law and general legal principles.

Setting out these constitutional fundamentals in an explicit document serves two purposes. First, it makes the structure of the Union and the values on which it is founded clear and understandable to citizens. Second, it allows the fundamental elements of the constitution to be strongly protected against change. Democratic constitutions usually prescribe a more difficult and elaborate procedure for amending the constitution itself than for enacting ordinary legislation. If constitutional reforms are made by representative bodies, special safeguards include requirements for supermajorities or multiple approvals. Alternatively, a national referendum may be called to approve a new constitution or a constitutional amendment. These safeguards are not surprising given that constitutions provide basic protection of fundamental rights, which is of key importance in democracies.

To protect constitutional principles, however, it is not sufficient merely to write them down in a document and prescribe a heavy procedure for changing them. Some prespecified and well-defined body must also enforce the principles and the procedure for change. Otherwise the principles may be eroded by ordinary legislative or executive decisions. Over time, such erosion can lead to significant changes in the constitutional principles themselves; that is, the generally accepted interpretation of a particular provision is changed, although the words of the text remain the same. This possibility is particularly important where the constitution provides a general power, such as that in Article 235 of the EC Treaty.[3] We therefore need to consider what the procedure for changing the constitutional fundamentals of the Union should be and the institutional mechanisms whereby specific bodies protect the constitutional fundamentals.

7.2.1 Procedures for constitutional change

The only existing procedure for explicitly changing the European constitution is to revise the Treaties. This has been done a number of times since the Community was founded by the original Treaties of Rome. Each enlargement has involved amending the Treaties and there were also important *constitutional* reforms of the institutional and budgetary arrangements of the Community in the 1960s and 1970s. The most important recent changes were the Single European Act (SEA) in 1986 and the Treaty on European Union – the Maastricht Treaty – signed in 1992.

The existing procedure for amending the Treaties on which the Union is founded is laid down by Article N of the Maastricht Treaty. It consists of three stages. First, the Council must decide to convene an intergovernmental conference (IGC) after consulting the European Parliament and, where appropriate, the Commission – the 1996 IGC, however, is expressly foreseen by Article N itself. Second, any change in a Treaty must be approved unanimously at the IGC. Finally, the new Treaty must be ratified by each state in accordance with its own constitutional requirements. In some states ratification is by the legislature; in others the new Treaty may or must be submitted to national referenda.

The so-called *passerelle* provisions of the Maastricht Treaty allow certain matters from the second and third pillars of the Union to be brought into the EC pillar without the need for an IGC. Unanimity and ratification by all member states in accordance with their respective constitutional requirements are still required, however. The main effect of these provisions is, thus, to enable specific changes to be made without creating an open agenda of other reforms.[4]

The unanimity requirement
The procedure for changing the Treaty is far more stringent than that required for constitutional change in most federal states. This reflects the view that the EU is not a federation, and that as an international treaty the Treaty on European Union must be agreed upon by all national governments participating in the Union. The unanimity requirement for changing the Treaties strongly protects national interests in the EU.

There are good reasons to retain the unanimity requirement for changing the European constitution. One is that there is not enough political will in member states to transform the EU into a genuine federal state. The creation of all federations in modern history involved the centralization of armed forces. Defence and foreign policy are probably the public goods best provided at the central level of a state. They are also essential symbols and instruments of national sovereignty. If some countries do not want to commit to a common defence policy by transfer of national sovereignty, they are not prepared to undertake genuine political integration. Given this absence of political will, it is important to protect the interests of EU members that do not share the objective of creating a genuine federal state and do not want to transfer further sovereignty to EU institutions. The best protection is to maintain the unanimity rule for changing the Treaty. Another good reason for keeping the unanimity rule is that, by protecting the delimitation of the common base, it may induce agreement to greater use of majority rule in the ordinary legislative and executive processes of the common base in order to enhance the efficacy of decision-making.

If, however, the desire for integration deepens among member states, a case could be made for adopting rules for constitutional change like those that exist in most federal states. Unanimity has a definite cost in that all change is subject to the hold-up threat of any member state. This cost rises with the number of member states. Enlargement of the EU has, other things being equal, made change more difficult. Further enlargement will exacerbate the problem.

Legitimizing constitutional change
Unanimity does not ensure public acceptance of the legitimacy of Treaty changes. Nor does unanimous approval at an IGC guarantee easy ratification in each of the member states. The basic problem is that the negotiators at an IGC are the agents of national governments and only indirect representatives of citizens. The salient issues that lead voters to the choice of a national government may be quite remote from the issues that arise in negotiations about the transfer of powers to the European Union. Moreover, the positions taken by a government at an IGC may reflect only a temporary majority in that country.

For example, assume that, by coincidence, majorities in power in all EU states were to favour simultaneously the centralization of decision-making in Brussels. Although this is a highly unlikely event, it is possible to imagine these governments coming together and transferring national powers to the European Union. Such changes would not be perceived as legitimate, because the public would not have given them a mandate to do this in national elections.

A more realistic scenario is a multiplication of conflicts like those in former Yugoslavia east of the Union's current borders, resulting in military threats from parts of the former Soviet Union and very large flows of refugees. This might create strong cross-border coalitions, forming a clear European consensus for a common foreign and defence policy. In this situation, it would be important to have a legitimate procedure for expanding the common base to include such new competences.

The problem of finding a legitimate procedure for constitutional change is illustrated by the Maastricht Treaty. On the one hand, the negotiations resembled those for international treaties founding international organizations such as the World Trade Organization or the International Monetary Fund. On the other hand, the Maastricht Treaty was regarded as much more fundamental than an ordinary international treaty. In many states the ratification processes for the Maastricht Treaty recognized the relationship of democracy to constitutional change. It became the subject of profound political and constitutional debate and even of legal challenges. Governments submitted the Treaty to approval by popular referendum even when such a procedure was not mandated by the national constitution.

The problem was that this activity came too late, when the only possibilities were to accept or reject the package of changes that had already been agreed. Fundamental constitutional change at the national level involves public debate, either in constitutional assemblies directly elected by voters with a mandate to change the constitution, or by directly elected legislatures. An IGC has no such legitimacy and part of the public discontent with Maastricht concerned the absence of a mandate to negotiate a monetary union. It is not inconceivable to think that in some future period, voters would have a more direct say in the election of national representatives sitting at IGCs, thereby giving them more the flavour of constituent assemblies.

7.2.2 Institutions to protect the constitution

Appropriate institutional machinery is needed to ensure that the constitution of the Union is respected and that it is changed only by the proper procedures. The function of protection involves a number of separate tasks. Under flexible integration, one important task is to protect the principles of the common base. Another is to police the existing division of policy areas between the supranational common base and the intergovernmental open partnerships.

Protecting the principles of the common base

Up to now the main guardian of the constitutional principles enshrined in the law of the Community has been the Court of Justice. Recent critics of the Court have accused it of being too activist and of going beyond the proper interpretation of Community law to pursue a political agenda of further integration. These criticisms are misconceived. Constitutional courts always have a role in deciding what the constitution is as well as in protecting it against violation by other institutions. The Treaties are unusual in that they are both more complete and more incomplete than most written constitutions. As noted in Chapter 2, they contain details normally found in the ordinary laws or administrative regulations of a state. At a constitutional level, on the other hand, the Treaties are silent on many important matters of principle, perhaps because the full implications of the integration to which member states agreed were not understood at the time. A good example is the relationship between national law and Community law. The Treaties say nothing, but the Court of Justice has had to resolve disputes about the matter. Its decisions in favour of the supremacy and direct effect of Community law were justified, because these decisions best fit the logic of integration which the member states themselves initiated through the Treaties setting up the Community. Calls for judicial restraint imply a theory of judicial deference, that is, that the Court ought to leave the decisions in question to other institutions.[5] In practice, however, the member states as *Masters of the Treaty* have not taken the opportunity to undo the Court's work at IGCs.

The Maastricht Treaty (Article L) largely excludes the Court of Justice from the domains of the common foreign and security policy (CFSP) and justice and home affairs (JHA), the second and third pillars of the Union. The exceptions, however, are interesting. The first concerns the JHA pillar, which permits the adoption of conventions about certain matters. Such conventions may provide for the Court to have jurisdiction under arrangements to be laid down by the convention itself (Article K.3.2 (c)). The member states thus have the discretionary power to give the Court jurisdiction and to decide on its terms. The second exception concerns Article 228a of the EC Treaty, which allows the Council to take measures to impose sanctions on a third country when doing so has been agreed under the CFSP pillar. Although Article 228a does not say so expressly, the Court of Justice necessarily has jurisdiction to interpret and examine the legality of such measures, because the Article is part of the EC Treaty. Similarly, if the *passerelle* provision of the JHA pillar discussed earlier is used, the matters concerned would automatically come under the jurisdiction of the Court.

With flexible integration, a similar distinction could be drawn. Open partnerships could confer jurisdiction on the Court, if the participating states chose to do so. The Court would, however, automatically have jurisdiction in so far as any action by an open partnership affected the principles of the common base. It would be useful to have a provision analogous to Article 228 of the EC Treaty, which provides for the Council, the Commission or a member state to obtain the opinion of the Court on whether a proposed international agreement between the Community and a third party is compatible with the Treaty. If the Court gives an adverse opinion, the agreement may enter into force only through the procedure for amending the Treaty.

Policing the limits of the common base

Under flexible integration, the distinction between the common base and the open partnerships is of fundamental constitutional importance, because they embody different modes of integration. New policy areas could be brought within the common base if the members of the Union so wished, but only through the process of Treaty amendment in which each state has a veto.

Policing the limits of the common base would thus be a new and very important function. What kind of body should carry it out? The possibilities are a political body, a judicial body, or a body which has a mixture of both characteristics. The main problem with using a political body such as the Council or European Council would be to ensure that a clear distinction is drawn between the constitutional decision that a proposed action falls within the policy areas of the common base and the political decision that the action in question is desirable. Without such a distinction, those who disagree with particular decisions are unlikely to accept their legitimacy.

The above discussion suggests that a wholly political body would be less appropriate than a judicial or a mixed body. The choice between the two depends on how the common base is delimited. The more vague and incomplete are the principles – for example, subsidiarity – the more political the policing function becomes. The more the common base is defined by rules containing a precise and exhaustive catalogue of competences, the more judicial is the policing function.

If the choice falls on a judicial body, there would be two possibilities. Either the Court of Justice could be the tribunal of competences, or a new body could be set up. Giving the function to the Court of Justice would have the advantage of avoiding legal complexities that could arise in defining separate jurisdictions. Furthermore, there is no doubt that the Court of Justice would strive properly to discharge a new mandate. The constitutional architecture of the Union might be more transparent and understandable for the citizen, however, if the separate functions of protecting the principles of the common base and policing its boundaries were performed by separate institutions.

Preventing interference by open partnerships in the common base

Policing the boundaries of the common base may be a more or less judicial function, depending on how precisely and completely the contents of the base can be delimited. In contrast, preventing the open partnerships from disrupting the proper functioning of the common base involves political judgement on the basis of economic and other policy evaluations which are likely to involve some risk and uncertainty. For example, it might be necessary to decide whether a proposed environmental or social policy partnership would create barriers to trade and, if so, to evaluate whether the likely gains would outweigh the risks it would present. The European Council, which under the Maastricht Treaty has the function of providing the Union with political guidance and impetus for its development, seems best placed to make the necessary decisions. To do so, however, it will need inputs from the perspective of both the Union and the member states. The Commission has the necessary expertise to perform this task. It also has an institutional interest in both protecting the common base and promoting further integration, so there is no reason to fear that its analysis would be biased either in favour of, or against, a proposed new partnership. It would also be appropriate for the European Parliament to have a consultative role, since this would acknowledge the interest that individual European citizens have in the Union as a whole, whether or not their state is to participate in a proposed partnership.

7.3   Decision-making in the European Union

We turn now to an evaluation of the current decision-making rules of the EU, as spelled out in the Treaty of Rome and the subsequent revisions. The discussion is conducted from the perspective of the common base and based on the three objectives for political constitutions outlined in section 7.1. We discuss in turn efficacy and adaptability, protection and representation of minority rights, and accountability.

7.3.1   Efficacy and adaptability

Lack of efficacy and adaptability are currently the two most visible institutional problems facing the EU, especially in relation to enlargement.

One of the main concerns regarding efficacy is the danger of paralysis in decision-making. This is, to a large extent, related to the size of required majorities. Majority rule may run from simple majority, to absolute majority, to unanimity. The smaller the required majority, the smaller the compensations required to buy off the votes of potential losers from policies that increase the overall efficiency of EU policies. As we discussed in the examples in Chapter 3, unanimity requirements may block decisions that are beneficial to a large majority and only mildly harmful to a small minority of the member countries. The unanimity rule may thus give rise to substantial hold-up behaviour by such minorities. It also puts decision-making at risk of irrationality or misperception: a member that mistakenly believes that it will lose from a decision may block an efficiency-enhancing decision.

In contrast, as the Marquis de Condorcet realized in his famous Jury-theorem, individual mistakes are likely to cancel out in the use of majority rule. On the other hand, majority rule may also lead to inefficient outcomes, imposing what Alexis de Tocqueville referred to as *the tyranny of the majority*. A majority may, for a small gain to each of its members, undertake a project that is very harmful to a minority. As the number of member countries increases, the risk of a tyrannical majority becomes smaller relative to the risk of a tyrannical minority of one. Protection of small minorities is, however, less important in decisions related to current management compared with decisions on constitutional change. This is because the constitutional definition of the competences is in itself the most important protection for minorities. Also paralysis of more routine decision-making for the given competences can be very costly. If countries value more protection of their sovereignty in some competences, however, majority qualifications may vary with the competences.

As discussed in Chapter 2, the most important decisions are presently made by the Council, with unanimity, qualified or simple majority. Even though majority voting increased in the 1980s and the Luxembourg compromise is less often invoked, unanimity voting remains the rule for any important decision within the European Union, be it the adoption of a new policy or the nomination of the President of the Commission. Consensus is also often sought even when majority voting is allowed. This is a result of the intergovernmental mode of decision-making. *De facto*, single countries retain veto powers when they feel strongly about a subject. The result is that the Council often finds it difficult to change the *status quo*. Naturally, the problem is bound to worsen with enlargement, because it will increase the heterogeneity of the Union.

The lack of a legal hierarchy is another important factor that tends to worsen the lack of adaptability. As the Treaty contains not only basic values, definitions of powers and rules, but also detailed provisions which, in normal legal frameworks, would be properly regulated by administrative decree, changes in small details of the Treaty require a revision of the Treaty and a full-fledged ratification process. This carries the danger of potentially opening the Pandora's box leading to demands to renegotiate the whole Treaty. Policy-makers are thus reluctant to propose even small changes that could be beneficial to all.

7.3.2 Protection and representation of minority interests

Constitutions of democracies define the allocation of powers and competences in order to protect fundamental rights of citizens, minorities and groups, and to prevent abuse and predation by government bodies. In particular, constitutions explicitly limit the powers of political institutions by introducing major institutional safeguards against unilateral action by single government agencies or bodies. This is assured by the separation of powers and systems of checks and balances instituted to protect interests of various minorities.

The predominance of the Council in decision-making has allowed national interests to be well represented in the EU so far. Council members are ministerial level representatives of individual states and the process of coalition-making in the Council tends naturally towards coalitions among countries. Protection of the interests of individual nations was reinforced by the unanimity rule and the search for consensus. If efficiency in decision-making requires less unanimity and more majority rule, the protection and representation of individual nations becomes an important issue. This raises the question of how to weigh the population of member states. The current allocation of votes in the Council gives each country votes roughly proportional to the logarithm of population (Widgrén, 1994). This tends to favour small countries. Belgium and Greece together have the same number of votes in the Council as Germany, whereas their joint population is less than one-fourth of Germany's. With future enlargement, a mechanical application of these weights to new entrants would dilute the power of large countries further (Baldwin, 1994). These countries will, therefore, advocate changes in the weighting scheme in their favour. Small countries such as Belgium, Luxembourg and the Netherlands, however, will not readily accept such changes, since they would reduce their relative influence in the Council.

As discussed in Chapter 2, weights in the European Parliament are more representative of country populations. But an increase in the powers of the European Parliament would still give Germany more power than France, as both countries have ten votes in the Council and Germany has 99 Euro-deputies compared with 87 for France. No wonder many French politicians are reluctant to give more powers to the EP and would prefer to see the Council's power extended.

More use of majority rule raises the question of how to protect national interests, but it is equally important to represent and protect interests that cross national boundaries. The predominance of the Council implies that in those areas where decision-making has moved from unanimity to majority, voting in the Council still promotes only coalitions of countries. The possibility of forming cross-border coalitions of groups with similar interests are therefore severely limited. This gives too much importance to national interests and does not allow aggregation of interests along border-cutting dimensions such as socioeconomic interests, environmental policies, women's interests, and so on.

For example, decision-making in the Council naturally leads to transfers or compensations to countries rather than to individuals. National politicians may find it politically profitable to campaign against paying transfers to other countries. Politicians who advocate pan-European interests will tend to be pushed into the background. The resulting need to find a compromise between national interests in all European matters makes Council decisions more difficult, and leads to stalemate. This leaves only the Commission and the European Parliament as places to build border-cutting coalitions. Even inside the current EP, however, border-cutting coalitions are unlikely to form. One reason for this is that its members are currently elected on country lists under country-specific electoral rules which differ widely across member states. Country loyalties tend to remain stronger than loyalty to European political groups. Without cross-border coalitions, pan-European interests, which presumably should be the

Box 7.1 The value of cross-border coalitions

Politicians in two nations, A and B, campaign to get elected on the basis of policies providing public goods. Assume there are four possible choices: (i) to produce only public good A, which is much desired in nation A, but which imposes a negative externality on country B; (ii) to produce only public good B, which is much desired in nation B, but which imposes a negative externality on A; (iii) to produce both A and B; (iv) to produce a good F, which represents a compromise. The citizens of A prefer having only A to having only F, having only F to having both A and B, and the latter to having only B. The citizens of B prefer having only B to having only F, having only F to having both A and B, and the latter to having only A. Even though they know that their preferred policy imposes negative externalities on the other country, it is in the interests of voters in each individual country to vote for *hardline* politicians who favour policy A (or B), because national interests will be better defended if a hardliner is elected in the other country. With hardliners elected in both countries, it may take them a long time to agree on both producing F. They may not even have an incentive to agree on this, since they can claim that failure to agree is the fault of the other country and get re-elected on a nationalist platform. The efficient policy F would have more chance of being implemented if voters from both countries could vote on a single district ballot. Politicians would have less incentive to push for policies A and B because it would cost them votes in the other country. There would be incentives for a border-cutting coalition to defend policy F.

foundation of an integrated Europe, thus have quite limited possibilities of forming and shaping the future of European integration.

Another important concern with respect to protection of minority rights is the distribution of agenda-setting powers inside European institutions. Agenda-setting power is defined by the right to set the agenda for proposals put to vote without being subject to amendments in the proposals or their order of adoption. A government's agenda-setting power is best illustrated by its power to put questions to vote through a referendum as in France, in contrast to referenda in Switzerland which can be initiated by citizens. Giving agenda-setting power to government bodies reflects the necessity to avoid paralysis in decision-making and to obtain the advantage of expert knowledge. In all democracies important agenda-setting powers are typically conferred on parliamentary committees, independent agencies and the executive.

Agenda-setting powers can exert considerable influence on collective choice. Say, for example, that a wide variety of new safety standards were acceptable to appropriate qualified majorities of participating states. If the Commission could propose one form on a take-it-or-leave-it basis, it could propose whichever form it liked best, subject to the acceptability constraint.

As described in Chapter 2, the Commission has the right of initiative in all the decision-making procedures of European institutions. It is responsible for drafting proposals as well as redrafting proposals amended or rejected by the European Parliament. The Commission, therefore, has quasi-monopoly over agenda-setting power. Only the co-decision procedure, introduced with the Maastricht Treaty, weakens its monopoly over the agenda.[6][7] This power of the Commission has had two important consequences so far. First, the Commission has played an important role in fostering European integration. Being the advocate for pan-European interests, the Commission has used its agenda-setting power to advance the cause of economic integration. Second, its agenda-setting power has been combined with little accountability to European citizens, creating a real danger for capture by special interests and for unwarranted tendencies to increase its powers and domains of competences. With increased accountability of the Commission, there would be less danger of its agenda-setting powers being abused.

7.3.3   Accountability

Direct elections are the most common way to achieve accountability of political decision-makers. Politicians seeking to remain in office have an incentive to defend the interests of their constituencies. In all countries the legislature is elected directly. In some countries elections are also held for the executive and, more rarely, a portion of the judiciary. The European Union holds direct elections only for the European Parliament. In many countries there is a large element of protest voting over domestic politics in these elections, with little focus on European issues. As illustrated in

Table 7.1 Election turnouts (%)

Country	Most recent general election	General election turnout	EP election turnout, 1989	EP election turnout, 1994
Belgium	21/5/95	83.7	90.7	90.7
Denmark	21/9/95	83.4	46.2	52.5
France	28/3/93	68.9	48.7	53.7
Germany	16/10/94	79.1	62.3	60.1
Greece	10/10/93	81.5	79.9	71.2
Ireland	25/11/92	68.5	68.3	44.0
Italy	28/3/93	86.4	81.5	74.8
Luxembourg	12/6/94	87.4[a]	87.4	86.6
Netherlands	3/5/94	78.3	47.2	35.6
Portugal	6/10/91	68.2	51.2	35.6
Spain	6/6/93	77.2	54.6	59.6
United Kingdom	9/4/92	77.7	36.2	36.4
Total			58.5	56.4
Sweden	18/9/94	86.8	–	41.3[b]

[a] General election 1989. [b] Election 18 September 1995.
Sources: Electoral Studies 1992: 2, 4; 1993: 2; 1994: 1, 2, 4; *Keesings Contemporary Archives* October 1991; April 1992; March 1993; March, May, October 1994; *Svenska dagbladet* 18 September 1995.

Table 7.1, voter turnout is often low (Gallagher, Laver and Mair, 1995). To some extent this reflects the general perception that the European Parliament's power is largely irrelevant. Parties often select their candidates for these elections accordingly, with a low proportion of national heavyweights.

The two key agents in the European decision-making process, the Commission and the Council, are emanations of national governments not accountable to EU citizens through direct elections. In principle, a government can be punished in national elections for decisions or appointments approved by the Council. This happens very rarely in practice, partly because of lack of information but mainly because of the bundling of responsibilities. A national government will mainly be judged on how it deals with domestic policies in national elections. Consequently, its behaviour in the Council is not often subject to scrutiny by the electorate at large.

Currently, individual Commissioners are named by national governments. Big countries often send to the Commission one representative from the majority and one from the opposition. Therefore, it is often said that Europe is governed at the centre. In the political sense governing from the centre may be desirable, but the elite consensus represented in the Commission may also be out of touch with the public. As a bureaucracy insulated from the electorate, the Commission may favour policies that strengthen its role, pushing for an excessive amount of regulation and subsidy. At a large distance from the ballot box, it may be more easily captured by the special interest groups it subsidizes and regulates.

Because of this lack of accountability, it is more difficult to control moral hazard by national governments and the Commission. Moreover, decision-makers are more easily captured by lobbies and interest groups. Only the groups and individuals most affected by the EU decisions may find it worthwhile to acquire information and lobby the Commission or the national governments. Thus EU decisions may be more responsive to special interests and less responsive to the general interests.

The lack of accountability of the Council and the Commission directly relates to the ambiguity of the transfer of competences from member states to the EU. The logic of intergovernmentalism clashes with the principle of direct elections of European political institutions because direct elections give these institutions an unambiguously supranational character. The cost of this ambiguity has, however, been a lack of accountability.

This ambiguity is enhanced by the confusion of responsibilities between the Commission and the Council. Some policy decisions are *de facto* taken by the Commission, not by the Council. Moreover, the Commission's agenda-setting power gives it considerable influence over Council decisions. The fuzziness in the respective responsibilities of the Council and the Commission makes it even more difficult to hold one institution or the other accountable to European citizens.

Granting citizens the right to check government action by standing in the courts is also an important means of promoting accountability. As seen in Chapter 5, individual citizens and companies can submit complaints to the Commission (Article 169 TEU) or raise actions in national courts (Article 177). The Maastricht Treaty also recognizes the citizens' right of petition, that is, to submit petitions to a special committee in the European Parliament on any matter within EC competences. The Parliament may then use its influence to bring a case concerning a member state to Court. The Parliament may also elect an ombudsman for a five-year term. As discussed in Chapter 5, however, there are limitations to these possibilities.

To summarize, the current decision-making process has serious deficiencies: the lack of accountability of key decision-makers, the incomplete representation of cross-border interests and diffused general interests, and the inefficient *status quo* bias resulting from the reluctance to accept majority rule in the Council.

7.4   Suggestions for reform

The previous discussion suggests that institutional reform inside the common base should reduce the democratic deficit by moving simultaneously in the following directions: enhanced efficacy through the extension of majority voting to all policies that are part of the common base; more direct accountability of EU decision-making to European citizens; and the promotion of cross-border coalition formation and a better balancing of the interests of large and small countries. Institutional reforms should be seen as packages. Because of the important complementarities between reforms, individual reforms have different effects depending on which other reforms are adopted simultaneously.

There is no unique reform package moving in the directions mentioned above. Rather than proposing a single reform package, we discuss two scenarios which differ mainly with respect to the role of the Commission: one with the Commission as an executive and the other with the Commission as an administration. We discuss in particular how, despite important differences, these two reform packages can be constructed in a way to enhance simultaneously efficacy, accountability and a better balance of representation.

7.4.1   The Commission as an executive

The main elements of a reform package under this scenario are the following:

- Extending majority voting inside the Council and introducing double majority rule in the Council, one according to the existing number of votes in the Council, and one according to the population size of countries.

- More monitoring of Council decisions by national parliaments.

- Maintaining, or even reducing, the number of Commissioners, and making this number dependent on a fixed number of functional competences, rather than rules for country representation.

- Maintaining the Commission's current right of initiative but extending it to the European Parliament.

- More direct accountability of the Commission to the European Parliament by giving it the right to vote down the Commission by simple majority through a constructive vote of confidence.

- Moving towards a bicameral system of decision-making where European legislation requires approval of both the European Parliament and the Council.

- Delegating specific enforcement powers of the Commission to independent agencies.

- Introducing a harmonized electoral system for the European Parliament where each voter receives two votes, one for a local representative on a majority ballot at the level of a district (as in the United Kingdom and in the German first vote), and one on a pan-European proportional ballot (as in the Netherlands) with a threshold (say 5% as in Germany) required for representation.

- Maintaining the number of members of the Parliament at its current level, even after enlargement.

How does this package meet the three objectives defined above?

More efficacy is obtained by putting a limit on the number of Commissioners, by separating the Commission's missions of agenda-setting and enforcement of Community legislation, and by introducing more majority voting in the Council.

The current system of selecting the Commission, which allows each nation at least one Commissioner, becomes less practical as membership grows. Moreover, it signals to the public and to national governments that the European executive is busy mainly with finding compromises among national interests rather than being a truly European policy-making body.

We mentioned in Chapter 5 the potential conflicts of interests arising from the Commission's multiple missions in enforcement of the Single Market. Probably one of the biggest tensions arises from the Commission's dual role as the agent responsible for the enforcement of Community decisions and as advocate for Europe, making proposals to deepen European integration. This may give rise to inefficient outcomes where the Commission would, for example, be ready to buy acceptance by member states for certain legislative proposals in exchange for lax enforcement of existing Single Market legislation. The example in section 3.3.3 can also be interpreted in this way. The solution to that conflict in this scenario entails delegating enforcement powers to independent agencies.

Increasing the scope of majority voting inside EU institutions will be at the heart of the discussions at the 1996 IGC. Debates on majority voting in Europe are really proxies for debates on the transfer of national sovereignty to Europe. Federalists will thus appeal to the need for efficacy, whereas anti-federalists will appeal to the need for representation of national interests and protection of national sovereignty. We argue in this Report that flexible integration provides a solution acceptable to both camps. More majority decision-making is easier to accept in a narrow set of policy areas inside the common base. The areas with the largest disagreement are left outside the common base, and subsets of countries will still be free to pursue common policies by means of new open partnerships. Sovereignty over those competences that are part of the common base, however, have to be unambiguously transferred from the nation states to the European Union. Decisions on the form of majority rule should be revised before, or simultaneously with, any further enlargement of the Union.

Introducing more majority procedures in the common base without any further changes, however, is likely to make the democratic deficit an even more burning issue, both because Council decisions exclude the formation of cross-border coalitions and because the Council and the Commission lack direct accountability. The reform package considered also increases the accountability of the Council and the Commission by increasing the role of national parliaments in monitoring decision-making in the Council, by extending the Commission's right of initiative to the European Parliament, and by making the Commission more accountable to the European Parliament.

Suggestions to increase the role of national parliaments in monitoring Council decisions are welcome in that respect. The Danish Parliament's standing committee on EU matters – which has an important role in influencing the agenda and positions taken by Danish ministers in the Council – is often cited as a positive example. It is, however, worth noting that changes in domestic procedures are not substitutes for reform of the European institutions in addressing the democratic deficit. Indeed, closer scrutiny of the Council by national parliaments, in addition to carrying the risk of being relatively impracticable and, therefore, increasing the *status-quo* bias in the Council, can only strengthen the representation of national interests in the EU. It does not contribute to a better representation of cross-border interests. The same reasoning leads us to reject proposals making the Commission directly accountable to national parliaments. Reform in this direction would worsen efficacy by drastically increasing rigidity and delay in decision-making, and increase the representation of national interests to the detriment of cross-border interests. Making the Commission accountable to the European Parliament is a better solution, because it leads to more efficacy and a more balanced representation of interests.

Enhancing the accountability of the Commission is very important to reduce the democratic deficit, given the important agenda-setting powers of the Commission. To preserve the Commission's role as advocate for European interests and to simplify decision-making by the Council, its right of initiative ought to be preserved. But there is no convincing reason why the Commission should retain a monopoly. On the contrary, it is important to consider new mechanisms for generating competition in the formulation of proposals by also giving initiation powers to the EP. As discussed in Chapter 3, allowing for decentralized integration incentives in the form of new open partnerships will also bring some competition into the agenda-setting process.

Increased democratic legitimacy for the Commission, as an executive, can go either in the direction of parliamentary democracy, the dominant form of government in Europe, or in the direction of a presidential system, where there is direct election of the executive. In the former case, the European Parliament must be given the power to vote down the Commission by simple majority rather than the present two-thirds majority of votes cast. Such a vote of no confidence should be constructive, however, in that the Parliament must agree on a replacement Commission first.

In the latter case, the executive would serve a fixed term between two elections, as in the US system. Proposals for direct election of a European executive are currently remote from the agenda, but could become appropriate if policies like defence and foreign policy become part of the common base, implying that important powers be given to the executive. Without such powers, efficacy in decision-making requires that, as an agenda-setter, the Commission commands a majority in the European Parliament, which points more in the direction of a parliamentary system, whereby the executive is accountable to the elected parliament.

A better balance of representation is obtained by a double majority in the Council and adequate electoral reform in the European Parliament.

As such, the Council reflects the aggregate interests of countries and coalitions among countries. Since it is important to protect these interests, the Council should certainly remain a central pillar of European institutions. However, as discussed above, the Council protects national interests at the cost of giving small nations disproportionate weight. It is possible to correct this distortion without unduly decreasing the power of small countries by introducing a double majority rule in the Council, one according to the number of votes in the Council, protecting interests of small countries, and one according to population, protecting interests of large countries. The cost of such a rule is that it favours the *status quo*. If, however, double majority rule goes together with a reduction in unanimity voting, the overall *status-quo* bias would still be reduced. Thus more efficacy could be achieved while protecting the interests of small and large countries.

We mentioned above that Council decisions reflect only national interests. In addition to inadequate protection of within-country minorities, having coalitions only of nations hampers efficient decision-making. To correct this distortion, it is important to introduce political incentives for border-cutting coalitions to defend European-level issues in the Parliament which is directly elected by European citizens. A bicameral system (EP plus Council) protects national interests (through votes in the Council) as well as cross-border coalitions (in the EP).

Increased accountability of the Commission to the European Parliament will maintain its role as an advocate for Europe, provided the Parliament becomes the locus for cross-border coalitions. This can be fostered by appropriate electoral reform. Currently, members of the EP are elected according to different rules set in each country. There should be a harmonization of rules. EP elections should give European citizens representation of their local interests *vis-à-vis* 'Brussels' and at the same time encourage cross-border coalitions. Such an electoral reform would have the following features. Each voter would have two votes, one for a local representative on a majority ballot at the level of a district, and one on a pan-European proportional ballot with a threshold (say 5%) required for representation. The second vote would give parties incentives to form cross-border coalitions, which would be further encouraged by the threshold for representation. Members of the EP elected in the proportional ballot would constitute half the seats and those elected from regional ballots would constitute the other half, but other combinations can be considered.

At the same time, it is important to keep the number of representatives in Parliament to a reasonable number and to avoid inflation in the number of Euro-MPs with enlargement. Keeping a fixed number of representatives increases accountability and transparency, since too many representatives reduces the possibilities for voters to be informed and monitor the behaviour of their representatives.[8]

Note that the proposal to give each voter two votes for the same parliament is not the same as introducing a parliament with two chambers. With two chambers, decisions by the two groups would be taken in sequence, whereas with one composite chamber decisions would be taken simultaneously. The latter procedure enhances the scope for coalition-building.

Electoral reforms like these do not *per se* imply an expansion of the powers of the European Parliament. There has already been an increase in the power of the EP through the SEA. Further changes are required if EP elections are to be politically relevant at a European rather than national level. National governments themselves should have an interest in making EP elections more than a forum for negative views about domestic politics. Any reform giving more power to the European Parliament should clearly be combined with new EP elections before these powers can be exercised.

In what directions should the powers of Parliament be expanded? The cooperation and co-decision procedures introduce elements of bicameral decision-making which go in the right direction. Co-decision could be extended to all the areas where majority decision-making is accepted. This would make decision-making more democratic, more efficient and also more transparent, since a single procedure would replace the current structure with multiple procedures. The co-decision procedure could, however, be further simplified by requiring a majority vote in the EP and in the Council to get proposals adopted. Such a majority rule in both chambers would then protect national as well as cross-border interests.

7.4.2   The Commission as a European administration

This scenario contains the same elements as the previous one except that the role of the Commission would be confined to that of an administration responsible for the enforcement of the common base and for managing the interactions between open partnerships and the common base. The Commission's right of legislative initiative would be maintained only inside the competences of the common base. It would, however, have gate-keeping authority over legislation proposals inside these competences, that is, the possibility of blocking proposals unless a stronger majority (say of two-thirds) can be found to adopt them. The Commission's unique expertise in coordinating policies between member states would also be used fruitfully by making its administrative services available for the management and coordination of open partnerships.

It would be less necessary to delegate the Commission's enforcement powers to independent agencies.[9] So far the administrative role of the Commission as an executive has been limited, as national administrations are responsible for the bulk of the implementation of European policies. In this scenario, the Commission's powers and capacities – or that of separate agencies – would be expanded, in particular in monitoring enforcement of Community legislation.

Removing the Commission's right of initiative risks bringing the process of European integration to a halt unless another, equally strong advocate for Europe is created to provide an adequate balance between national and cross-border interests. Without the role of the Commission, the Single Market is unlikely to have become a reality. In this second scenario it is, therefore, crucial to designate another EU institution to be an advocate for Europe, drafting legislative proposals for that purpose and playing the role of an agenda-setter. To have democratic legitimacy, such a body should emanate from the European Parliament, the only existing directly elected European institution.

Agenda-setting powers would be delegated to the European Parliament. More specifically, a committee for initiating legislative proposals, equipped with adequate staff to maintain the quality of proposals currently formulated by the Commission, would be chosen from within the European Parliament and be able to command a majority there. Here also the introduction of a constructive vote of no confidence would avoid paralysis in agenda-setting.

Increased accountability of the Commission could be achieved by giving the EP the power to confirm nomination of individual Commissioners. Even if almost no nominations would be rejected, anticipation of the confirmation process would still influence the decisions. Furthermore, it could be achieved by giving the EP the power to impeach Commissioners for malfeasance in office.

Some reform proposals in the current debate deny the Commission any role as an executive and want to concentrate more power in the Council, as is the case with the second and third pillars of Maastricht. Transferring power from the Commission to the Council would not only reduce representation of European interests compared with national interests, but also make European institutions even less accountable. After enlargement, Council meetings would have so many participants that they would increasingly resemble the meetings of a legislative body. The Council would have to appoint a smaller body – like a permanent secretariat or a Council presidency – as reflected in some recent French proposals. This body would play more or less the same role as the Commission today, yet again with many layers of delegation and little accountability.

7.5   Conclusion

We have discussed in this final chapter institutional aspects of managing a European Union under flexible integration and reducing the democratic deficit in the European decision-making process.

Under flexible integration there would be new roles for the European Court of Justice and for the Commission. The former would have automatic jurisdiction over open partnerships in so far as they affect principles of the common base. It could also have jurisdiction over the partnerships themselves, if the participating countries so wish. The Commission would be a watchdog for the common base and check that open partnerships do not interfere with its proper working.

Reforms in political decision-making must lead simultaneously towards more efficacy and adaptability, more direct accountability of EU bodies and a better balance of representation. Major reforms include more majority voting in the Council with a double system of weights, electoral reform for the European Parliament to encourage border-cutting coalitions and more power for the Parliament. Moreover, the enforcement and agenda-setting powers of the Commission should be separated. Two different scenarios for reform of the Commission were discussed from that perspective.

Although the reforms considered above may appear to advance supranationalist or federalist objectives, our motivation is practical. Given past enlargements and anticipated future enlargement, we view the current institutions as inadequate for realizing the gains from the integration process initiated by the Treaties of Rome and continued, via the Single European Act, through the Maastricht Treaty. Anti-federalists should be reassured by the fact that our analysis in this chapter is essentially directed at a more narrow slice of the current activities of the EU, namely those included in the common base. Integration and coordination outside the common base, through the creation of open partnerships, is still left to unanimous, intergovernmental negotiation among the participating countries. Thus the reforms are very much in line with the historical evolution of the EU discussed in Chapter 2: to narrow the policy domain of deep integration but to accept a bigger transfer of sovereignty over that domain.

Federalists, on the other hand, may object that any reform of the Commission, even with additional powers for the European Parliament, may have the unintended effect of killing all options for future deepening of European integration. We are conscious of the necessity of a proper balance inside the European institutions between the advocates of national interests and the advocates of European interests and consider that the latter should not be weakened but rather strengthened inside the common base. Any reform of the Commission should, therefore, be considered in conjunction with proposals for increasing the powers of the European Parliament and reinforcing its role as an advocate for European integration. Thus proposals for change should be seen as a package and not be evaluated in isolation.

Notes

1. See Dixit (1995, Chapters 1–2) for a similar and more extensive discussion of constitutions as incomplete contracts.

2. Accountability is the duty of an individual or institution to explain and justify its behaviour. It necessarily involves the possibility of criticism if the performance revealed by the account is judged unsatisfactory. Accountability may also include liability to more formal sanctions, to the withdrawal of delegated authority, or to greater control and monitoring of future behaviour.

3. 'If action by the Community should prove necessary to attain, in the course of the operation of the common market, one of the objectives of the Community and this Treaty has not provided the necessary powers, the Council shall, acting unanimously on a proposal from the Commission and after consulting the European Parliament, take the appropriate measures.'

4. See Article K.9 of the Treaty on European Union and Article 100c of the EC Treaty.

5. The Council presidency also has some agenda-setting powers, in that it can ask the Commission to draft proposals. Similarly, the Commission does not have the power to present the Council and EP with unamendable, 'take-it-or-leave-it' proposals: the Council can always amend proposals. However, in the consultation and cooperation procedures (see the description in Chapter 2), the Council can amend Commission proposals only by unanimity. The Commission's monopoly to draft proposals gives it enormous power to frame subsequent debates.

6. For discussion of this point in relation to similar criticisms of the US Supreme Court made by President Nixon, see Dworkin (1977) Chapter 5.

7. Note, however, that in the cooperation procedure, interests of the European Parliament can be forwarded by the Commission. If a proposal of the Commission is amended by the Parliament and the Commission agrees with these amendments, the Council can

amend this proposal only by unanimity whereas it can adopt the proposal by a qualified majority.

8. Note the elections to the US Senate, which has only 100 members, are very competitive, with only modest advantages to incumbents. In contrast, re-election rates of incumbents almost always exceed 90% in the House of Representatives, which has 435 members. The lack of competitiveness in House races stems only partly from the relative homogeneity of House districts. It is also a consequence of television technology and advertising costs.

9. See, however, Chapter 5 on the advantages of agencies with simple missions.

References

Alesina, Alberto, and Vittorio Grilli (1992), 'The European Central Bank: Reshaping Monetary Politics in Europe', in Canzoneri, Matthew, Vittorio Grilli and Paul Masson (eds.), *Establishing a Central Bank in Europe: Lessons from the US*, Cambridge University Press, Cambridge.

Alesina, Alberto, and Vittorio Grilli (1993), 'The European Central Bank: Reshaping Monetary Politics in Europe', in Canzoneri, Matthew, Vittorio Grilli, and Paul Masson (eds.), *Establishing a Central Bank: Issues in Europe and Lessons From the US*, Cambridge University Press, Cambridge.

Baldwin, Richard (1994), *Towards an Integrated Europe*, Centre for Economic Policy Research, London.

Balladur, Edouard (1994), 'Pour un nouveau traité de l'Elysée', *Le Monde* 30 November.

Begg, David *et al.* (1991), 'The Making of Monetary Union', *Monitoring European Integration* 2, Centre for Economic Policy Research, London.

Ben-David, Daniel (1993), 'Equalizing exchange: Trade liberalization and income convergence', *Quarterly Journal of Economics* 108, pp. 653–80.

Bocquet, Dominique (1994), *Ce que la France doit repondre a l'Allemagne*, Mouvement Européen France, Paris.

Bolick, Clint (1994), *European Federalism: Lessons from America*, The Institute of Economic Affairs, London.

Bolton, Patrick, and Gérard Roland (1995), 'The Break-up of Nations: A Political Economy Analysis', mimeo, ECARE, Université Libre de Bruxelles, Brussels.

CDU (1994), 'Überlegungen zur europäischen Politik', CDU/CSU Fraktion des Deutschen Bundestages, mimeo, Bonn.

Coe, David T, and Reza Moghadam (1993), 'Capital and Trade as Engines of Growth in France', International Monetary Fund Staff Papers, pp. 542–66.

Collinson, Sarah, Hugh Miall and Anna Michalski (1993), 'A Wider European Union: Integration and Cooperation in the New Europe', Discussion Paper 41, Royal Institute of International Affairs, London.

Commission of the European Communities (1991), 'The Development and Future of a Common Agricultural Policy', (MacSharry Report), COM (91) 258 Final/3.

Commission of the European Communities (1995a), *Douzième Rapport Annuel sur le Contrôle de l'Application du Droit Communautaire*, COM (95) 500 Final.

Commission of the European Communities (1995b), *The Single Market in 1994*, Report of the Commission to the Council and the European Parliament.

Cooter, Robert, and Josef Drexl (1993), 'The Logic of Power in the Emerging European Constitution: Winners and Losers Under the Maastricht Treaty', mimeo, Brussels.

Cremona, Marise (1994), 'The "Dynamic and Homogeneous" EEA: Byzantine Structures and Variable Geometry', *European Law Review* 19, pp. 509–26.

Daintith, Terence (1995), 'The indirect administration of Community law', in Daintith, Terence (ed.), *Implementing EC Law in the United Kingdom: Structures for Indirect Rule*, Wiley Chancery Law, Chichester.

De Grauwe, Paul (1994), 'Towards European Monetary Union without the EMS', *Economic Policy* 18, April.

Dehousse, Renaud, and Joseph H H Weiler (1990), 'The legal dimension', in Wallace, William (ed.), *The Dynamics of European*

Integration, Pinter Publishers, London, for the Royal Institute of International Affairs.

De Ruyt, Jean (1987), *L'Acte Unique Européen*, Editions de l'Université de Bruxelles, Brussels.

Dewatripont, Mathias, and Gérard Roland (1992), 'Economic Reform and Dynamic Political Constraints', *Review of Economic Studies* 59, pp. 603–30.

Dewatripont, Mathias, and Gérard Roland (1993), 'The Design of Reform Packages under Uncertainty', Centre for Economic Policy Research Discussion Paper No. 860.

Dewatripont, Mathias, and Jean Tirole (1995), 'Advocates', mimeo.

Dixit, Avinash (1995), *The Making of Economic Policy: A Transaction Costs Politics Perspective*, MIT Press, Cambridge, MA.

Dworkin, Ronald (1977), *Taking Right Seriously*, Duckworth, London.

Eichengreen, Barry (1990), 'Is Europe an Optimum Currency Area', Centre for Economic Policy Research Discussion Paper No. 478.

Electoral Studies, various issues.

European Parliament (1994a), *Report of the Committee on Institutional Affairs on the Constitution of the European Union*, Doc EC\RR\244\244403, 27 January, mimeo.

European Parliament (1994b), 'Minutes of the sitting of Thursday, 10 February 1994', mimeo.

Fratianni, Michèle, and Jürgen von Hagen (1992), *The European Monetary System and European Monetary Integration*, West View Press, Boulder.

Gallagher, Michael, Michael Laver and Peter Mair (1995), *Representative Government in Modern Europe*, McGraw Hill, New York.

Gerbert, Pierre (1994), *La Construction de l'Europe*, Imprimerie Nationale, Paris

Giavazzi, Francesco, and Alberto Giovannini (1989), *Limiting Exchange Rate Flexibility*, MIT Press, Cambridge, MA.

Gibson, James L, and Gregory A Caldeira (1995), 'The legitimacy of transnational legal institutions: Compliance support and the European Court of Justice', *American Journal of Political Science* 39, pp. 459–89.

Grossman, Sanford, and Oliver Hart (1986), 'The Costs and Benefits of Ownership: A Theory of Vertical and Lateral Integration', *Journal of Political Economy* 94, pp. 691–719.

Hart, Oliver (1995), *Firms, Contracts and Financial Structure*, Oxford University Press, Oxford.

Institute of Directors (1994), *A New Agenda for European Prosperity*, London.

Italianer, Alexander (1994), 'Whither the Gains from European Economic Integration?', *Revue Economique* 45, pp. 689–702.

Jacquemin, Alexis (1990), 'Horizontal concentration and European Merger Policy', *European Economic Review* 34, pp. 539–50.

Keesings Contemporary Archives, various issues, Keesings Ltd, London.

Keohane, Robert, and Stanley Hoffman (1991), 'Institutional Change and Europe in the 1980s', in Keohane, Robert, and Stanley Hoffman (eds.), *The New European Community: Decision-making and Institutional Change*, West View Press, Boulder.

Laffont, Jean-Jacques, and Jean Tirole (1993), *A Theory of Incentives in Procurement and Regulation*, MIT Press, Cambridge, MA.

Lamfalussy, Alexandre (1995), 'The Harmonization of Monetary Policy in Europe: What Steps and When?', mimeo.

Leiderman, Leonardo, and Lars E O Svensson (eds.), *Inflation Targets*, Centre for Economic Policy Research.

Lodge, Juliet (1987), 'The Single European Act and the New Legislative Cooperation Procedure: A Critical Analysis', *Journal of European Integration* 11, pp. 5–28

Lohmann, Suzanne J (1994), 'Federalism and Central Bank Autonomy: The Politics of German Monetary Policy, 1957–1992', mimeo, University of California at Los Angeles.

Lucas, Robert (1988), 'The Mechanics of Economic Development', *Journal of Monetary Economics* 22, pp. 3–42.

McCubbins, Mathew D, and Thomas Schwartz (1984), 'Congressional Oversight Overlooked: Police Patrols versus Fire Alarms', *American Journal of Political Science* 28, pp. 165–79.

McCubbins, Mathew D, Roger G Noll and Barry R Weingast (1987), 'Administrative Procedures as Instruments of Political Control', *Journal of Law, Economics and Organization* 3, pp. 243–77.

Molle, Willem (1994), 'The Economics of European Integration', Dartmouth Publishers, Brookfield, Vermont (2nd edition).

Neven, Damien (1994), 'The Political Economy of State Aids in the European Community: Some Econometric Evidence', Centre for Economic Policy Research Discussion Paper No. 945.

Neven, Damien, Robin Nuttall and Paul Seabright (1993), *Merger in Daylight: The Economics and Politics of European Merger Control*, Centre for Economic Policy Research, London.

Nurske, Ragnar (1949), *International Currency Experience*, League of Nations, Geneva.

Pentland, Charles (1973), *International Theory and European Integration*, Faber and Faber, London.

Persson, Torsten, and Guido Tabellini (1993), 'Designing Institutions for Monetary Stability', Carnegie Rochester Conference Series on Public Policy.

Persson, Torsten, and Guido Tabellini (1994), 'Federal Fiscal Constitutions: Risk Sharing and Redistribution', mimeo, IGIER.

Persson, Torsten, and Guido Tabellini (forthcoming), 'Federal Fiscal Constitutions: Risk Sharing and Moral Hazard', *Econometrica*.

Persson, Torsten, and Guido Tabellini (1995), 'Double edged Incentives: Institutions and Policy Coordination', in Grossman, Gene and Kenneth Rogoff (eds.), *Handbook of International Economics* 3, North Holland.

Pinder, John (1995), *European Community. The Building of a Union*, Oxford University Press, Oxford (new edition).

Piris, Jean-Claude (1994), 'After Maastricht, are the Community Institutions More Efficacious, More Democratic and More Transparent?', *European Law Review* 19, pp. 449–87.

Putnam, Robert (1988), 'Diplomacy and Domestic Politics: The Logic of Two-Level Games', *International Organization* 42, pp. 427–60.

Sala-i-Martin, Xavier, and Jeffrey Sachs (1992), 'Fiscal Federalism and Optimum Currency Areas: Evidence for Europe from the United States', in Canzoneri, Matthew, and Paul Masson (eds.), *Establishing a Central Bank: Issues in Europe and Lessons from the US*, Cambridge University Press, Cambridge.

Stigler, George J (1971), 'The Theory of Economic Regulation', *Bell Journal of Economics* 2, pp. 3–21.

Tsoukalis, Louka (1977), *The Politics and Economics of European Monetary Integration*, George Allan and Unwin, London.

von Hagen, Jürgen (1995), 'Inflation and Monetary Targeting in Germany' in Leidermann, Leonardo and Lars E O Svensson (eds.), *Inflation Targets*, Centre for Economic Policy Research, London.

von Hagen, Jürgen, and George Hammond (1994), 'Regional Insurance Against Asymmetric Shocks in a European Monetary Union', Centre for Economic Policy Research Discussion Paper No. 1170.

von Hagen, Jürgen, and Manfred J M Neumann (1994), 'Real Exchange Rate Variability Within and Between Currency Unions – How far is EMU?', *Review of Economics and Statistics* 76, pp. 236–44.

Wallace, William (1990), 'Introduction: The dynamics of European integration', in Wallace, William (ed.), *The Dynamics of European Integration*, Pinter Publishers, London, for the Royal Institute of International Affairs.

Walz, Uwe (1995), 'Dynamics of Regional Integration', mimeo, University of Mannheim.

Webb, Carole (1983), 'Theoretical Perspectives and Problems', in Wallace, William, and Carole Webb (eds.), *Policymaking in the European Community*, John Wiley and Sons, New York (2nd edition), pp. 1–41.

Weiler, Joseph H H (1991), 'The transformation of Europe', *Yale Law Review* 8.

Whiteley, Paul F (1994), 'Comment: Is European Integration Stalled?', Abegaz, Berhanu, Patricia Dillon, David H Feldman and Paul F Whiteley (eds.), *The Challenge of European Integration*, West View Press, Boulder.

Widgrén, Mika (1994), 'Voting Power in the EC Decision-making and the Consequences of Two Different Enlargements', *European Economic Review* 38, pp. 1153–70.

Wilson, James Q (1991), *Bureaucracy*, Basic Books, New York.

Wissenschaftlicher Beirat beim Bundesministerium für Wirtschaft (1994), 'Ordnungspolitische Orientierung für die Europäische Union', mimeo.

Wyatt, Derek, and Alan Dashwood (1993), *European Community Law*, Sweet & Maxwell, London.